PUNCTUATION BOOK

PENTAGON PRESS
DELHI INDIA

PUNCTUATION BOOK

***First Published* : 2004**

ISBN 81 86830 30 8

Published by :

PENTAGON PRESS
101, AVG Bhawan,
M-3, Connaught Place
New Delhi - 110 001
INDIA
91 11 2332 1198, 2341 5205, 91 11 51517091

Printed at :
Elegant Printers
New Delhi

PREFACE

Punctuation is a part and parcel of a writer's profession and it is equally important for a layman as well. Though many of us are still unaware of the correct usage of the punctuations – the apostrophes and the hyphens – we like to use it in our writings. Appropriate usage of punctuation comes with practice and time.

To create awareness among the masses over the correct usage and the importance of punctuations, 'Pentagon's Punctuation Book' has been specially designed. It consists of almost all the rules and regulations one probably might have been unaware of. The book teaches the perfect usage of the question marks, full stops, semicolons, colons, exclamation marks, contractions etc.

The book provides indepth usage the signs and symbols. All the usages are well supported by appropriate examples, which makes the understanding a lot easier. The correct usage of quotations is also provided. Moreover, the significance of italicizing the words and making it boldface is also emphasized upon.

Overall, 'Pentagon's Punctuation Book' is the perfect medium through which you can learn how to jewel your writings with the proper usage of the punctuations.

CONTENTS

CHAPTER 1

A GUIDE TO PUNCTUATION

People very often wonder at the need to learn proper punctuation. It is a well-known fact that a number of people have earned fame and prestige without ever knowing the correct way to place a semicolon or an apostrophe. Often people say that punctuations are merely decorative patterns in a piece of writing that do not need to be paid any attention to. Some people also regard punctuation as an exercise of personal rights- if you want to use it, then do so, if you do not want to use it, then don't.

Putting punctuation aside for the moment, let's examine the other parts of the written English language. There are a number of words that are pronounced alike but have different spellings. But would you write 'seam' for 'seem' because you think that the first one would look nicer? Or would you write, "The homies are a bunch of freggin' lunatics," because that is the way people around you talk? Similarly would you write 'expect' for 'except' because you have really never understood the difference between them? I do not think so.

Everyone wants what they are writing to be correct and exact. Then the punctuation too should be faultless. It is however very possible that you are writing very common and obvious mistakes in your compositions that can be corrected with a bit of increased knowledge in the area of punctuations.

Maybe, you use commas where you just feel like and are not aware of the method behind it. Perhaps you never really understood what a semicolon was meant to do. Maybe you just put the punctuations where you feel like because you never took the time to find out what to put where. Maybe you think that punctuations are a waste of time because the words are more important and people don't need punctuations to understand what you are saying. But punctuations can drastically alter the way your work will be read, as you shall soon find out.

As a matter of fact, badly put punctuation marks can confuse the reader as to what you are trying to say. Why should the reader then waste his or her time reading a piece of writing that may not be understood by him or her at all. The reader will expect you to follow correct grammatical patterns and punctuation marks. No one likes to read something that will be an enigma from the start to the end.

English is a language that uses all sorts of equipment to make the meaning of what is being said very clear. We can use: stress, rhythm, pause, intonation, etc. Even repetition and alliteration, etc are the oft-used tools of the English language. But when we are speaking most of these apart from the two last ones are useless to us. We cannot read out what we have written. Then the labor that they perform in speech is handled entirely by punctuation in the written article. Then we realise that English has set up a very strict code for using punctuation and anyone who writes in English and wishes to write well will have to learn this code. In this system all punctuation marks have their role to play and should only be used in that light and not in any arbitrary manner that pleases you. if

> The parliamentary committee's decision to introduce a new women's bill has provoked angry outbursts from the conservative sections, effigies have been burnt.

Henry won the races each year, this year he lost to Mike.

These examples are all made up of two distinct pieces of information, which have been clubbed without any attention being paid to the punctuation marks. In all the sentences either the sentences should be separated by a full stop or they should be linked by 'and' or 'whereas'.

For a different method of punctuating such sentences look to Chapter 4 where you will learn to use semicolons for such sentences.

Summary:

- Place a full stop at the end of a sentence.
- A comma cannot connect two distinct statements.

HOW TO USE THE QUESTION MARK

A question mark (?) is also placed at the end of a sentence. The distinction between this and a full stop is that a question mark can only end a sentence that asks a direct question. For example:

What time is it?

> Who took the cookies from the cookie jar?
>
> When can I get an increase in my allowance?
>
> Did Salman Rushdie write '*Midnight's Children*'?

In which part of the world do we find igloos?

If the sentence is a direct question quotation, wherein the speaker is being quoted, then too you will use a question mark. For example:

She asked me, "Do you really think that Brad Pitt is cute?"

"Where are the toilets?" he asked the receptionist.

"Can I sign up for classes on feminism?" he inquired.

But if the speaker is not being quoted verbatim and the question is not directly conveyed, you cannot use the question mark. For example:

She wanted to know if I had stolen her pen.

He asked if he could still join classes on feminism.

She asked me if I really thought that Brad Pitt was cute.

Sine the whole sentence is a statement, a question mark will not be used. Instead, we will use a full stop.

The question mark can also be used to indicate an uncertainty about something. If it is put between parentheses, it shows a doubt over what has been mentioned. For example:

Shakespeare (1576? – 1616) wrote *Loves Labour Lost* in 1597 (?).

Hardy claimed that he knew the language *teern absidd* (?) that was spoken by aliens from mercury.

The question marks indicate that there is no surety about the information that has been given. Shakespeare birth year is undecided as it is the year when he wrote *Loves Labour Lost*. They have been estimated to be the years stated but doubt or controversy still exists. In the second sentence, the language 'teern absidd' cannot be verified as true so a question mark indicates doubt over the authenticity of the claim being made.

Summary:

- A question mark is placed at the end of a direct question.
- An indirect question cannot be terminated by a question mark.
- A question mark can be used to convey doubt on a given matter.

HOW TO USE THE EXCLAMATION MARK!

The exclamation mark (!) is placed at the end of a sentence that conveys some strong feeling or expression. Given below are a few examples:

What a strange looking bird!

You are going to murder your boss!

Of course not!

Ouch!

Get away from that tiger!

I want to see the manager!

Lets party!

This punctuation mark is very useful when a story is being told. It is often used in novels and stories to convey a depth of emotion like shock or excitement. But formal writing has hardly any use for the exclamation mark.

If you make too much use of the exclamation mark, your writing sounds as if it is gasping or winded. It can also give your text a juvenile and immature quality.

The exclamation mark can also be used after sentences that start with a 'what' or a 'how'. For example:

> How idiotic you are!
>
> What crazy ideas keep rotating in your head!
>
> How dare you say that!
>
> What a sore loser!

If you notice you will realise that none of these sentences are questions or statements. They are all exclamations of some idea or feeling. See the difference in the quality of emotion if you remove the exclamation mark:

> How idiotic you are.
>
> What crazy ideas keep rotating in your head.

The exclamation mark can be used to indicate great surprise. For example:

> I worked all night to give the project in the next day. It wasn't the due date!
>
> She cautiously stepped over the bramble and peeped in through the window of the house. It was vacant!

An exclamation can also draw attention to an interruption. For example:

> The nest was empty (a rarity!) so we stole the eggs.
>
> The shock on his face (so obvious!) told us that he knew nothing of what had happened.

But refrain from using the exclamation mark in your formal writings. Do not indulge in sentences like:

> Avoid exclamations in your writings!

Do not be boastful!

The denim industry is expanding at a rapid rate!

Try not to use the exclamation until it is necessary for the purpose. And never use more than one exclamation mark for one sentence, no matter how strange, bizarre or shocking the news may seem to you. It is not grammatically correct to write:

How easy it is to use the exclamation mark!!!!!

Even if you use such a style in your informal writing, it is acceptable but never do so in any formal composition.

Summary:

- Avoid using the question mark until it is required.
- Use the exclamation mark after an exclamatory sentence, especially one that starts with 'what' or 'how'.

NOTE A FINAL POINT:

Remember that none of the above, full stop, exclamation mark or question mark, can be preceded by a blank space. It would not be correct to write:

How are you ?

This is wrong .

What you see is improper punctuation !

What would be correct would be the punctuation mark following the last word closely. For example:

How are you?

This is not wrong.

What you are seeing is proper punctuation!

WHAT TO DO WITH FRAGMENTS:

A fragment is a sentence or phrase that is written separately but does not make sense and cannot stand independently. These are often used in advertisements, newspapers, classifieds and even in ordinary everyday speech. If they are used in formal writing, their number should be as minimal as possible. They should then end with a full stop, question mark or exclamation mark as required:

Did she take her dog to the veterinarian? Hopefully.

Shall I ask her to have dinner with me? Why not?

Can Andre Agassi beat Patrick Rafter? Definitely!

If you can use the right amount and the right kind of fragments in your writing, then your writing can become more vibrant and intense. Never use too many fragments, as it can get repetitive and monotonous. The work can also seem winded and incoherent.

CHAPTER 3

HOW TO USE THE COMMA

The comma (,) is perhaps the most widely used (and often misused) punctuation mark in the English language. The ways of using a comma are very simple but the types of commas are four. That is to say, that a comma can be used in four different styles. The four categorical divisions are: *listing comma*, *joining comma*, *gapping comma* and *bracketing comma*. All three have distinct uses but keep in mind that a space cannot precede a comma and a space must always follow a comma.

THE LISTING COMMA:

This type of comma can be broadly described as an alternative for the word 'and'. It can be used in three different circumstances. Firstly it can be used when there are more than two words, phrases and sentences that are clubbed together with the words 'and' or 'or'. This can be called an A, B and C type of comma. Here are some examples of the listing comma:

> Goldilocks went to the forest, ate the pudding that belonged to the bears, tried out all the beds and fell asleep on the bed of the baby bear.

That night Julie, Christie, Mandy and I were frightened by the great storm that raged outside.

Monica likes fudge, Nina likes Chocolates, Nikita likes ice creams and I like pies.

We ate a heavy meal, drank some wine, went out for a walk and retired to bed feeling extremely happy.

You can choose your major from French, German, Spanish and Latin.

As you can see the commas can be replaced by 'and' or 'or' but the effect of such a change would be gauche and awkward. For example:

Monica likes fudge and Nina likes chocolates and Nikita likes ice creams and I like pies.

Goldilocks went to the forest and ate the pudding that belonged to the bears and tried out all the beds and fell asleep on the bed of the baby bear.

That night Julie and Christie and Mandy and I were frightened by the great storm that raged outside.

You can choose your major from French or German or Spanish or Latin.

Remember that you can use the listing comma for three or more different words, sentences and phrases. See the difference:

Monica likes fudge, Nina likes chocolate, Mandy likes ice cream but I like pies.

❖ Monica likes fudge, Nina likes chocolate.

You should never join two sentences with a comma. Only three or more sentences can be joined with a comma, besides 'and' and 'or'.

Also keep in mind that according to the British method you cannot place a comma before 'and' or 'or', though the American method does place a comma there. So if you are following the British pattern you cannot write:

> I love to eat cakes, fudge, and pudding.

Though it would be considered proper to do so in the American method. However, if you feel that placing a comma would make the sentence clearer you may do so. For example:

> My favourite musicians are Tina Turner, Phil Collins, and Marky Mark and the Funky Bunch.

Here if you had omitted placing a listing comma the fact of Marky Mark and the Funky Bunch being a music band would not have been as obvious as it is now. Then the sentence would have looked like:

> My favourite musicians are Tina Turner, Phil Collins and Marky Mark and the Funky Bunch.

The meaning here is a bit more confused. One might think that Phil Collins and Marky Mark were a team whereas the Funky Bunch was another independent group. The listing comma can therefore be a very useful punctuation device.

A listing comma is used for a modifiers list if all the modifiers work on the same thing. If the comma is placed, an 'and' will not be needed and vice versa. But both can be used for the sentence to make sense. For example:

> It is a quiet, eerie spot.
>
> The dog was warm, cuddly, small and very lazy.

An 'and' can be added and the sense of the sentence would still remain the same.

It is a quiet and eerie spot.

The dog was warm and cuddly and small and very lazy.

Though the sense remains almost the same, the latter sentences are definitely more clumsy and awkward. Note the next few lines:

I love old English songs.

She has an antique silver brooch.

Here it would be wrong to place a comma between the descriptive words. For example, the following would be incorrect:

I love old, English songs.

She has an antique, silver brooch.

Why can a listing comma not be added here? The reason is very simple. There is no list here. As you can see the word 'and' cannot be used instead of the commas placed. The modifiers are not modifying the same thing here. 'English' modifies 'songs' but 'old' modifies 'English songs'. Likewise 'silver' modifies 'brooch' while 'antique' modifies 'silver brooch'.

Summary:

- A listing comma can be placed wherever 'and' can be used and nowhere else.
- Place a listing comma before 'and' or 'or' if it helps you to make your meaning clear.

THE JOINING COMMA:

There is a faint difference between the listing and the joining commas. The joining coma can join two entire sentences into one single sentence. So a suitable connecting word is very important for a joining comma. The words that can be used by a joining comma to connect two sentences are 'and', 'or', 'while', 'yet', 'whereas', 'but', etc. a few examples are listed below:

> I cannot say no, but I cannot say yes.
>
> I love to eat, and I love to swim.
>
> The month of June is hot whereas, the month of November is cool.
>
> I have had eight hours of sleep, yet I feel tired and sleepy.
>
> Give me the magazine, or give me the novel.

As I had stated earlier you cannot join two sentences if you are not using one of the connecting words. So the following sentences are all wrong:

> Ireland is a turbulent place, the IRA grows stronger each passing year.
>
> English are known for their naval excellence, the Israelites are known for their security excellence.
>
> I suggested going fishing, Harry wanted to go shopping.
>
> There are many bees in this area, I am terrified of bees.

This joining of two independent sentences with a comma is perhaps the commonest mistake in punctuation. However if you keep a look out for it it is one of the easiest to avoid. There are two available options. Either you use one of the connecting words listed below or you substitute the comma with a semicolon as explained in Chapter 4.

Also keep in mind that most connecting words cannot follow a joining comma. Such connecting words are: 'however', 'nonetheless', 'thus', 'hence', 'therefore', etc.

So the following sentences are all wrong.

I felt that he was cheating me, however, I could do nothing about it.

I researched all night, thus I had the material on time.

Writing a dictionary is not an easy business, nonetheless, I am going forward with this.

It rained all day long, hence, we stayed at home and watched a movie.

We know now that these sentences do not require a comma but a semicolon as explained in Chapter 4.

Summary:

- A joining comma is used to join two entire sentences using words like 'and', 'hence', 'yet', etc.

THE GAPPING COMA:

A gapping comma is used to indicate that some words have been left out, when the words would have merely been repeating words that have already been stated within the sentence. For example:

A few of the villagers wanted to elect Rashid as their head, others Abdul.

What is missing from the latter part of the sentence is the same information that has been stated earlier- 'wanted to elect'. Otherwise the sentence would have been longer:

A few of the villagers wanted to elect Rashid as their head, others wanted to elect Abdul as their head.

Here is another example:

> Beethoven is remembered for his musical compositions, Leonardo da Vinci, for his inventions, Van Gogh, for his paintings, and Michelangelo, for his sculptures.

A listing comma has been placed to give a sense of clarity. Gapping commas are not always essential if the meaning is clear enough without it.

Beethoven is remembered for his musical compositions, Leonardo da Vinci for his inventions, Van Gogh for his paintings and Michelangelo for his sculptures.

You have to use your own reasoning as there are no clearly stipulated rules. If the sentence makes perfect sense without the gapping commas then avoid using them. If there is any doubt as to the meaning then use gapping comas.

Summary:

- A gapping comma is one which indicates that a few words have been left out that have already been stated.
- A gapping comma should only be used if the meaning of a sentence is not clear enough without it.

BRACKETING COMMAS:

They are also known as '*isolating commas*'. They are very different from the other commas so far. Yet they are used the most often and can cause more trouble if used wrongly than the other three. A bracketing comma will mark off as separate that part of the sentence that is not that essential for that sentence but which nonetheless has been placed there. That is to say they preserve a sense of smoothness and continuity in the sentence. Note that a bracketing comma will never be used singly but in pairs. Though sometimes one of the pair will not be written as we explain below. Here are some examples of bracketing commas:

> Simon and Garfunkel, a sensational singing duo, are my favourite singers.
>
> Quasimodo, though very deformed, had a loving heart.
>
> After my results, which were not so good, I had to drop out of school.
>
> During his years in the army, of which he spoke very little, my grandfather was very heroic for which he won a national medal for bravery.
>
> James Dean, though he died really young, managed to go down in history as a memorable character.
>
> Schindler, a high class German, still helped the Jews who were being persecuted in Hitler's Germany.
>
> The young man, who had fallen in love for the first time, felt like he was on cloud nine.
>
> We have decided, after a long and careful deliberation, that none of us have any reasons for keeping you out of the committee.

You will notice that in every sentence the more unnecessary piece of information has been bracketed in by the help of commas. You will also realise that in each sentence the bracketed off section could be removed from the sentence without any damage to the sentence itself. For example:

> Simon and Garfunkel are my favourite singers.
>
> Quasimodo had a loving heart.
>
> The young man felt like he was on cloud nine.
>
> After my results I had to drop out of school.

This is always how bracketing commas function. It is a device to check our punctuation. If on checking your sentence you find that if you remove the bracketing comas the sentence is likely to collapse then there has been some mistake in the sentence construction. For example here is a wrong use of bracketing commas:

> As I looked, I saw a stray dog, and felt very sad for him.

We know this is wrong because if we take out the bracketed phrase 'I saw a stray dog' we are left with 'As I looked and felt very sad for him' which needless to state is incomplete and sounds ridiculous. This is an improper use of the bracketing comma because 'I saw a dog' is not incidental to the sentence but is very essential for the sentence to make any sense. The easiest way to correct this mistake is to simply remove the bracketing commas. For example:

> As I looked I saw a stray dog and felt very sad for him.

Now the sentence makes perfect sense. Here is an example:

> He fumbled around for his pen, and having found it, began to write.

Again the result is strange. If you remove the bracketed words 'and having found it' you are left with 'he fumbled around for his pen began to write.' This is again incomplete. This time there is a weaker section of the sentence but it is only 'having found them'. 'and' is integral for the sentence to maintain a coherent logic. So we shift the first comma a bit behind:

> He fumbled around for his pen and, having found it, began to write.

So now when the brackets are removed the sentence still makes perfect sense:

He fumbled around for his pen and began to write. (that he found the pen is automatically assumed).

Many people get very confused about bracketing comas so we shall look at many other examples to help you understand it better.

Sheila was a hard, even cruel woman.

What is the problem here? We know that that comma cannot possibly be a listing comma, a joining comma or even a gapping comma; hence it is probably a bracketing comma. But where does the interruption lie? The first few words 'Sheila was a hard' cannot be the weak part of the sentence because it introduces the subject. The interruptive part here is 'even cruel'. Thus the bracketing commas should e placed like this:

Sheila was a hard, even cruel, woman.

This is now a perfect sentence for if we remove the bracketed part it still makes sense:

Sheila was a hard woman.

Sometimes this mistake is not too obvious or complex so it passes by unnoticed but at other times wrong bracketing can lead to very confusing results:

> The Third Partition of Poland was the last, and undeniably the most mortifying event in the sad fall of the once dominant empire.

Here the fragment before the comma ('The third partition of Poland was the last') can make sense by itself but with just one comma it ends up sounding as if the third partition of Poland was the last one. Then it seems as if 'undeniably' starts another sentence which has been joined to this first one. So when you reach the end of the sentence you are left wondering what you missed and have to reread it to make sense of it. This is an indication of bad writing. The way to solve this problem would be to add another comma:

> The Third Partition of Poland was the last, and undeniably the most mortifying, event in the sad fall of the once dominant empire.

The sense is now clear. Here is another example of bracketing gone wrong:

> The natives of Pakistan, who are dependant upon the import of beauty products, are protesting the rise of the Wall Street market.

Read without the bracketed bit it still is a proper sentence but somewhere down the line we have lost the meaning of it. We were not talking about all the people of Pakistan protesting but only a certain section that was affected by the fall of the market. So the sentence is not actually correct:

> The natives of Pakistan are protesting the rise of the Wall Street market.

So the weak bit of the sentence is actually essential for it to retain a bit of truth. It adds the truth quotient to the sentence:

> The natives of Pakistan who are dependant upon the import of beauty products are protesting the rise of the Wall Street market.

This is now correct. We have removed the bracketing comma because we were not actually talking of the entire populace of Pakistan but a few of them, the ones that depend upon the import of beauty products for their livelihood. So the phrase 'who are dependant upon the import of beauty products' is not incidental to the statement but is an integral part of it. Therefore here we do not need bracketing commas.

What we have observed in the last two examples are two types of clauses: the restrictive (defining) relative clauses and the non-restrictive (non-defining) relative clauses. A restrictive clause is one that identifies what is being talked about and hence can never be bracketed off. A non-restrictive clause does not identify the subject being talked about but adds information to what has been said hence it is usually placed in bracketing commas. Given below are certain examples of both types of clauses. Let us first see the non-restrictive clauses:

> My aunt, who hates dogs, refused to let our dog near the kitchen table.
>
> The neighbours, who are always prying into our lives, wanted to know where we were going for the holidays.
>
> Toni Morrison, who is a black feminist author, has recently published a book called 'Playing in the Dark'.
>
> Ogden Nash, who died sometime ago, wrote some of the most hilarious poetry I have ever read.
>
> The restaurant, which was the best a year ago, went into a sudden decline and had to be shut down in the space of four months.

As you will see the non-restrictive clauses, that have been bracketed, can easily be removed without any alteration to the sense of the sentence. These only give added information, which is not really needed for our understanding of the sentence.

Now we will observe the restrictive relative clauses:

> The money that was the last of their resources was also stolen from them.

> Anyone who has seen the pictures of the aftermath of war can never support such a destructive procedure of solving issues.
>
> My belief is that though we are only humans prone to erring we have a great strength within us that will always point out the right path to us.
>
> This time when we sat on the merry go round I fell off.
>
> People who think that existentialism is the answer to life's issues are deluding themselves.
>
> Robin Hood had he not been a good man would have made it hard to justify his actions.

If there were no restrictive clauses here the reader would not have clearly understood what you were talking about. Even the sentences that might otherwise be correct will not carry any logical statement with them. For example w would have had 'Had Robin Hood would have made it hard to justify his actions'. This is wrong. A major chunk of the sentence is missing leaving us with half an idea of what is being said.

A proper name always identifies a person so it is hardly ever precedes a restrictive clause. For example:

> I met Justin Andrew who was a good friend of mine during my school years.

Here the clause that follows the proper name should be bracketed off. An exception to this rule is when 'the' precedes the proper name of a person for that indicates that the person being discussed was situated in a particular stage of time at the moment we are talking about. For example:

The Nathaniel that I had known ever since I was a child was not the same Nathaniel who returned from the war a wounded, broken and embittered man.

Remember that 'that' can only be used to usher in a restrictive clause, so a relative clause cannot then be bracketed off. For example:

The college authorities, that had been discussing the matter for an hour, declared that a decision was yet to be reached.

If this sentence is used to identify the college authorities then the commas should be removed. If not, then the 'that' should be removed and be replaced with a 'which'.

Often a feeble and interruptive part comes at the start or at the end of a sentence. It is not possible to bracket the part then. What you do is to simply drop one or the other of the bracketing commas. But you can never place a bracketing comma either at the start or end of a sentence. Then either the first comma is placed after the interruptive part or the second comma is placed before the interruptive part. For example:

All said and done, I think I can sing better then she can.

I think I can sing better than she can, all said and done.

This way when the bracketing comma is at the beginning than the last comma is dropped and when the latter comma is placed the earlier comma is dropped. If the interruption is at the middle then:

I think, all said and done, that I can sing better than she can.

So the interruption now can have two bracketing comas. But no matter where the interruption is placed the sentence retained its basic logic. The only difference was in tonal quality. The following list contains sentences with interruptions at the beginning and at the end:

At the beginning:

> Unlike his uncle, Sam never learned to get over his fears and was a very cowardly chap.
>
> After the meal, the little children went out to play.
>
> Besides Mary, no one else could tolerate the temper tantrums that John occasionally threw.
>
> Having exercised already, I was very reluctant to take my dog out for a walk.
>
> Although I like him, it is very tough for me to be able to for give him for what he has done.

At the end:

> The rain did not cease all day, as I had foretold.
>
> I liked the side dish of pork chops, as they were tender.
>
> During the night I heard a strange noise that was coming from the kitchen, as far as I could make out.
>
> We went for a trip to New Orleans, where the people are very friendly.
>
> I love to go out for a walk with my dog Vladimir, who is a Bloodhound.

As you can see the words after or before the bracketing commas can be easily removed without any damage to the coherency or logic of the sentence. Read out the sentences without the clauses and see.

There are quantities of general words that on average establish feeble interruptions that hold entire sentences. Some of the most common ones are: *although, though, even though, because, since, after, before, if, when* and *whenever.* Feeble interruptions launched by such words are as a rule quite extended, and as a result they mainly appear at the start or at the conclusion of a sentence. Here are a few examples:

> Although India has very recently begun promoting sports like tennis, they are already a great crowd attraction.
>
> After he had left the house, Sheila and the children felt very defenceless and scared.
>
> If I find you playing in water again, I am going to report you to your parents.
>
> The British lasted a very long time in India, because here they were welcomed as guests and treated with respect.

There is one more case where you might find that you have used bracketing commas incorrectly. Read the following sentence and try to figure out why the bracketing commas are wrong:

> Remember that in each one of these instances, the matter situated off by commas may well be detached exclusive of changing the sentence.

Here the comma given in this example is obviously not a listing comma, a joining comma or a gapping comma. Can it be a bracketing comma? Try eliminating the words before the comma:

> The matter situated off by commas may well be detached exclusive of changing the sentence.

The matter seems to be good enough so it seems to be a proper usage of the bracketing commas. It is not so. What was important in the earlier sentence was the instruction to 'Remember that' which is missing here. The interruption here is the words 'in each of these instances'. When we removed all that was before the comma we managed to remove apart that is very essential for the sentence. This means that the original punctuation was wrong. A correction should be made:

Remember that, in each of these instances, the matter situated off by the commas may well be detached exclusive of changing the sentence.

Now the interruption can be removed without any alteration in the original sense of the statement. Remember that it is only the bracketed part that can be removed. Nothing else should have to be changed.

So always be careful about the part that you are bracketing off. It really must be feeble and interruptive. Nothing that is essential to the meaning of the sentence should be bracketed off.

Often you will realize that what is feeble need not be necessarily bracketed off. So both the sentences listed below are okay:

> After the meal, I took a nap.
>
> After the meal I took a nap.

Even without the bracketing comma this sentence is very clear. Often though you have to use a bracketing comma to make everything clear. For example:

> When I was eating a snake came before me and I froze in mid action.

While reading this, the reader may think that I was eating a snake. So the sentence structure is at fault. This can be corrected by using bracketing commas:

> When I was eating, a snake came before me, and I froze in mid action.

Mistakes like these are common enough while you are writing. But if you wish to make your meaning clear then you must always reread what you have written. Just remember that a reader will not bother reading your material for long if at every sentence she or he has to pause and try to figure out what it is that you are trying to say.

Summary:

- Bracketing commas can separate a feeble part of the sentence from the main part.
- If the feeble part is at the end or the beginning then only one comma is used.
- The feeble part must surely be feeble and not have any essential elements init.

SUMMARY OF COMMAS AS A WHOLE:

There are four kinds of commas: listing comma, joining comma, gapping comma and bracketing comma.

A listing comma can be substituted by the words 'and' or 'or':

> I can eat meat, vegetables and sweets.
>
> I can eat meat and vegetables and sweets.
>
> You can go shopping, eat out or watch a movie.
>
> You can go shopping or eat out or watch a movie.

Joining Commas should precede connecting words like 'and', 'or', 'but', 'yet', 'while', etc.:

> The mail was due an hour age, and I am still waiting for it to come.

She tried to read a book, but her attention was not focused on it.

The train is a slower form of transport, while the airplane is much faster.

Gapping Commas show that some words have been omitted. These words are always ones that would have been repeated since they already are placed in the sentence:

I like my sister, and she me.

He walked down the alley whistling to himself, she didn't.

Bracketing Commas are used usually in pairs unless the feeble part is at the start or the end of the given sentence. They distinguish the main part of the sentence from the feeble part. The feeble part can always be totally removed from the sentence:

My grandfather, who hates modern music, has forbidden us to play Linkin Park.

The tiger, which was locked in its cage, looked like he had just had a very big meal.

If there is some doubt about how to place the commas you can ask yourself the following questions:

Can 'and' or 'or' replace the comma?

Do one of the connecting words (and, or, yet, etc.) follow the comma?

Does it indicate that repetition has been avoided?

Is the matter that is enclosed by a pair of commas, not really necessary?

If the answers to these questions are 'no' then something is not right in your sentence formation. See the following example:

> With the publication of her novel 'Beloved', Toni Morrison was launched into international fame.

Now ask yourself- can the comma be replaced by a 'and' or an 'or'? No. It will be illogical to do so. Does a connecting word precede the comma? No. is there a sense of something repetitive having been left out ? No. Since there is no bracketing off can it be a single comma usage of the bracketing comma? In that case can you leave out either the part before or the part after the coma? No. The sentence would be fragmented.

All the answers are no. Then we know that the comma does not belong there. Simply remove it:

> With the publication of her novel 'Beloved' Toni Morrison was launched in to international fame.

A listing comma is always used where it can easily be replaced by 'and' or 'or'.

A joining comma is placed before connecting words like 'and', 'or', 'but', 'while', etc.

A gapping comma is placed in a way that indicates the omission of a repetitive phrase within the sentence itself.

Bracketing commas are placed to enclose feeble and interruptive parts of sentences that are not really required.

CHAPTER 4

HOW TO USE THE COLON AND THE SEMICOLON

HOW TO USE THE COLON:

The colon (:) is regarded by many people as a difficult-to-place punctuation mark. But it is very easy to use since it has just one duty to perform. First things first: remember that a colon can never be preceded by a gap. It is, however, always followed by a single gap. A hyphen or a dash can also never be placed after the colon. It is very meaningless to use a dash or a hyphen after a colon.

What a colon does is to indicate that what ever is going to succeed is a more detailed, explanatory or listed form of what has thus far been written. The topic is then dealt on at length. Therefore it stands like this:

> Introduce the issue: detail the issue.

Usually a colon follows a complete sentence, though what succeeds may not be in sentence form. Sometimes it is a list in fragmented English and at time it can even be a word.

If you are following the British pattern refrain from capitalizing the first word after the colon. Though the American system often requires a capitalized word after the colon.

Here are some examples of how to use a colon:

> Venice is a great vacation spot: the architecture, the waterways and the people are all very warm and welcoming. (elaboration)
>
> I love spring: the flowers, fruits and the activity of natures other aspects gives life a zest that the other seasons cannot.
>
> One thing you must be wary of: If you do not exercise when you are young your body will be very weak by the time you are old.
>
> This much I know: I can never compromise quality for quantity.
>
> It was clear: one of us was the criminal and the trust that had existed between us was dangling by a very thin thread.
>
> Take this as a time-tested advice: never be late for any of your appointments for it often changes from a mistake into a habit.

Sometimes a colon will succeed the more detailed information:

> Love, food, music and wine: these are the things that can keep most people happy.

But this is an inversion and should not be used too often. Did you notice that the colon was never after a gap but always before one? Do not forget this simple but important fact.

Do not use a colon at the end of a heading of a chapter. If you see most books do not do so. A colon can be used for words, phrases and sentences when they are placed within a text. This is done to highlight what is going to follow.

The colon can also be used for some other purposes. If you are writing a book that has both a title and a sub-title, the you can use a colon to create a sense of difference between them. For example:

Have you read Harry Potter: The Prisoner of Azkaban.

Even though the original title may not be written with a colon but this is the correct way to write the title if you are referring to it.

The colon is used to cite passages from the Bible. The reading is taken from Romans chapter 6, verse 11.

It can also be used to write ratios: the division on the basis of gender in this class is 3:4 (boys: girls).

Though if you are writing a formal composition it would be best to put the ratio in words: the division on the basis of gender in this class is three to four where girls are in the majority.

The Americans use a colon when they write the time numerically: 11:45, 2:47, etc. But the British use a full stop: 11.45, 2.47, etc.

The last usage is the only time when colons are not succeeded by a gap.

See chapter 10 for the use of colons in formal letters and for referring to published texts.

HOW TO USE THE SEMICOLON:

The semicolon (;) has just one use- it can unite two separate sentences into a single sentence when the following circumstances are realized:

When the two separate sentences seem to be too closely linked to be put in separate sentences.

When a connecting word that requires a comma is not there.

A colon is also unnecessary.

This is an example:

> I like him; I hate him.

Not that the semi colon can be replaced by a full stop or even by an 'and'. Then the sentence could have read:

> I like him. I hate him.
>
> I like him, and I hate him.

But a semicolon shows that the two sentences are closer than usual. It gives a sense of a deeper relation than an 'and' would. But note that a semicolon has to be preceded and succeeded by complete sentences. There can not be any fragments when a semi colon is used. For example, here are a few wrong ways of using a semi colon:

> I hate him; a lot.
>
> The world was shocked at the most tragic event of the latter part this century; the death of mother Teresa.
>
> I think we have met before; maybe not.
>
> The shopping list grows longer; I have much to buy.
>
> After the collapse of the market; the depression set in for a long time.

All of these are incorrect. The semicolon cannot be used in this fashion when the two sentences are not really that close. Listed below are some correct ways of using a semicolon.

I am sure we have met before; it is at the back of my mind.

When you cry you cry alone; when you laugh the world laughs with you.

Boys like to gossip; girls like to play.

He is very fond of his family; he often goes home during breaks.

If a connecting word is used then you require a joining comma rather than a semi colon.

Boys like to gossip, whereas girls like to play.

However we should not forget that some connecting words are compatible with semicolons. These are: 'however', 'therefore', 'meanwhile', 'consequently', 'hence', etc.

People often express the opinion that aliens would be terrifying and cruel; however, I do not agree with this.

The people trapped under the bramble cannot be reached yet; meanwhile, rescue teams are proceeding as fast as possible.

We have yet to receive our salary; therefore we cannot afford to party right now.

You will realize that the part after the semicolon does stand as a entire sentence by itself. Also remember that however must be preceded by a semi colon. This is a very standard and oft repeated mistake.

There is one circumstance when a semicolon can be used to divide two sentences that are not complete. This is when a sentence has become too long and complex to survive on the separations afforded by commas only. At such times the semicolon can be placed at the more important pause, where the reader can get some space. See the following example:

> The deeds we do, the words we say, into still air they seem to fleet, we count them ever past; but they shall last, in the dread judgement they and we shall meet.
>
> - John Keble, *The Effect Of Example*.

The sentence is grammatically correct but the commas are so many that the sentence can get all muddled up in itself. If this is the case then the best thing to do is to place a semi colon where the greatest pause is. This preserves the coherence of the sentence and keeps it in a sentence without dividing it into two or greater parts.

But this sort of a use of the semi colon – the 'super comma' should not be very often used. It is better to divide up the sentence into two. Do not use either the semi colon (or indeed any other punctuation mark) as a tool for providing a gulp of air. Mostly the reader will know when she or he needs a break.

COMPARISON BETWEEN THE COLON AND SEMICOLON:

The semicolon and colon confuse many people. It will be good to contrast them here. For example:

> Nina was disappointed. Sam walked off in a huff.

It seems that the two sentences are not interlinked because of the full stop that has been placed between the two sentences. The only idea that strikes us is that people are unhappy though it is not linked to each other. Now we put a semi colon in that place and see:

> Nina was disappointed; Sam walked off in a huff.

Now the two sentences seem to be related to each other. Sam and Nina are probably upset over the same reason. A semicolon can only connect sentences that are linked already. Now we can place a colon and see the result:

Nina was disappointed: Sam walked off in a huff.

Similarly a semi colon also suggests a relationship between two sentences.

Summary:

- A colon is used to separate a broad topic from the details that follow.
- A semicolon can be used to join sentences that are not joined by any connecting words.

CHAPTER 5

APOSTROPHES AND CONTRACTIONS

HOW TO USE AN APOSTROPHE

The apostrophe (') is a tricky punctuation mark. It is often very confusing and often placed in the wrong place. There are many advertisements that tell you where to get *pizza's*, *haircut's*, *cream's*, *cold drink's*, *sweet's*, etc. Then there are other places that will tell you that they can provide *womens clothes*, *photographers cameras*, etc.

The confusion of the right way to place this punctuation is so great that many people have put forward the suggestion of abolishing the apostrophe as a whole.

However, you should not get your hopes up because the apostrophe is still very much part of the punctuation marks and doesn't show any signs of wilting under any sort of pressure. So try and learn it as well as you can.

A BIT ABOUT CONTRACTIONS:

Often the apostrophe has been used to write contractions. Contractions are shortened words from which an alphabet is missing. Usually these words are verbs and are very conventional words. Here are some of them with the original words:

It'	A has/it is
I'll	I will/ I shall
Shan't	shall not
Won't	will not
Didn't	did not
Don't	do not
They'd	they would/should
I'd've	I would/should have.

Remember that the apostrophe should be placed exactly where the displaced letter was. It is unacceptable to write *wo'nt* in place of *won't.* In the same way *I'd've* has two apostrophes in the omitted places. Remember that these sorts of contractions are very informal and should never be used for formal writings. Even in informal writings they should be used seldom otherwise it might get to be a habit. However, they are very useful for indicating accented speech and providing colour to a composition.

Mostly these contractions are a way of differentiating between words like *well* and *we'll.* There are many words that have been written with apostrophes for a very long time but are still regarded as incomplete words. But these are few and far in between. Here are some of them:

Hallowe'en Halloweven

O' clock of the clock.

Will o'the wisp will of the wisp

'tis it is

e'en even

Listed here are some of the common contractions used during speech.

Good mornin'

'Fraid so

's not fair.

It is best if you do not use such language in formal writing because it is still not accepted as proper. It is considered colloquial to use such contractions.

There is a vast difference between contractions and clipped forms. A clipped form is one that is arrived by the abridging a longer word. it is a very common tool of English speaking people. Here are some chipped forms:

gym	gymnasium
ad	advertisement
add	address
pro	professional
hippo	hippopotamus
bra	brassiere
abs	abdominal muscles
rhino	rhinocerous
flu	influenza
comp	computer
info	information
phone	telephone

These are not seen as contractions and should not be apostrophic.

APOSTROPHE USAGE:

Plurals:

Usually plurals do not require an apostrophe. So we will write words like *pizzas*, *creams*, *cold drinks* and *haircuts*. *Pizza's* would be a wrong word. as long as you are talking of singular thing, do not add an ' 's 'at the end. Even for proper names it is unacceptable to write 'Adam's' for 'Adamses'.

The British pattern calls for an 's' after the mention of dates like: I love the fashions of the 1980s. But the American pattern calls for 's': I love the fashions of the 1980's.

Possessives:

An apostrophe can be used to indicate a possessive noun, like Nina's money, Nathan's hair, Nikita's shoes. But remember that it is only the words that indicate a belonging (possessives) that use an apostrophe s ('s) at the end. For example:

Nina's knife	Jake's ruler	Rahul's son
Fool's garden	Andrew's family	Grandma's hat
India's culture	women's clothing	Ed's pen
My Life's story	His week's wages	Pam's pal

It is the same case even with words that end with an 's'. for example:

Dickens's novel	Adams's wife	Douglas's life
Bus's departure		

To this rule there are three exceptions. First is when a plural noun ends with an 's'. Then it will take only one apostrophe:

three weeks' pay my grandparents' anniversary the asses' ears

Since we do not pronounce such words with double *s* we do not write a double *s*. plurals without an *s* in the end take an apostrophe *s* in the end. Then proper nouns that end with an s take the apostrophe *s* only if the plural doesn't take an *s* as well. For example:

All saints' eve Ulysses' adventures

The third exception to this rule is when pronouns are concerned. See the following examples:

How is his back? This is hers.

Who wears these spectacles? Its paws were hurt.

The word 'its' never takes an apostrophe. For example this is wrong:

❖ The dog hurt it's ears.

This is one of the most obvious mistakes of the English language. It is often repeated and hardly ever recognized as a mistake. But know that you know that it is a mistake you can avoid it from your writings. It is a very easy fact to remember. The 'it's' that is used in English is never a possessive noun. You can say: it's raining. But that merely means that it is raining, not that the rain belongs to someone. This 'it's' is therefore a contraction of *it is* or *it has*. Also keep in mind that there is no word in the English dictionary as its'. This is totally wrong and should never be used.

Likewise, the possessive word *whose* can never be converted into *who's*. *Who's* is a contraction again. It means who is or who has. These two sentences are very different:

Who's your driver?

Whose diver is that?

One can be converted to *one's*. This goes to show that possessives can be apostrophic. But be careful about the word that you apostrophe. You cannot say 'the babie's clothes' because there is no such word as 'babie'. Then again you cannot name a store 'Baby's delight' because then it means that it is only one baby's delight. The correct thing would be to call it 'babies' delight'. It is, however, okay to say 'I like that baby's pram.' Here you are discussing a single baby.

CHAPTER 6

THE HYPHEN AND THE DASH

HOW TO USE THE HYPHEN:

The hyphen (-) is a small but useful tool of English punctuation. It can be used in a variety of ways. Mostly it shows that a word is being created out of two words. The hyphen can never have gaps either before or after it. One of the other most common ways of using a hyphen is to indicate that a word was too long to fit into the space provided and has been cut into two parts. For example:

> I am not aware of the reasons behind his staunch machia-
> vellian ideals.

Remember that you should not hyphenate words too much. If you do so, then try and keep the two parts as equal as possible. And try to break at obvious points. Do not be too abrupt. For example, the following will be wrong:

> Mach- machiavel-
>
> Iavellian lian.

These breaks are not equal and do not take into account syllable breakage. Many dictionaries carry words with hyphens. This will tell you how to hyphenate a word. If you are working on a computer you will probably have a word processor that will automatically hyphenate the word for you.

Whatever the case may be, make a note of the fact that a hyphen in such a use should be written at the conclusion of its line, and not at the commencement of the subsequent line.

The hyphen is also used while writing compound words, which, if not for the hyphen, would be vague, indistinct or stretched out. Then there is scope for person taste and opinions; however, definite rules may be acknowledged. Here they are:

Maintain a clear division

Avoid a hyphen unless necessary.

Try and stick to the rules laid down.

Always consult a good dictionary. If you are worried about the usage of words like space ship, space-ship or spaceship, then first of all go with your intuitions.

The British pattern favours the usage of hyphens whereas the American pattern usually works without them. If you are confused about these two, follow the third pattern and leave a gap between the words.

Sometimes a word can be too long to be put as one even though it would be grammatically correct to do so. Words like cobaltblue, are not incorrect but it is better to use cobalt blue.

The hyphen is also used for names that have double surnames like: Claude Levi-Strauss, Olivia Newton-John. But at times names like John Andrew Mayers, Helen Jones Smith do not do not use a hyphen. Then it is best to follow whatever the person prefers.

This is something vital: it is generally important to hyphenate compound modifiers. See the given examples:

She bid him good night's rest.

She wished him a good-night.

It is important to show the hyphen in the second line. The second good-night is a compound modifier. It has a slightly different meaning:

She wished him a good night.

The difference is subtle but present. Here are some other examples:

Her outfit is light yellow.

She's wearing a light-yellow outfit.

This cassette is worth twenty pounds.

This is a ten-pound cassette.

He constantly showed up for the revelry at the end of term.

He constantly showed up for the end-of-term revelry.

This paper is well thought out.

This is a well-thought-out paper.

His dog is five years old.

He has a five-year-old dog.

You can use hyphens as freely as you like in such compound modifiers; very often they are actually very essential for the meaning of the sentence to be well established: *a light yellow outfit* is not essentially *a light yellow outfit; the first-class vacation* is very dissimilar from *the first class vacation; a rusty-nail cutter* is distinct from *a rusty nail-cutter; a man-hating doctrine* is absolutely unlike *a man hating doctrine.* The reader can get a very different idea if you forget to hyphenate some of your words. For example see some of the differences of hyphenated and non-hyphenated words below:

A long-laid rule	a long laid rule
A time-tested friend	a time tested friend.
A well-defined system	a well defined system.
Little-expected help	little expected help
A green-eyed girl	a green eyed girl
A true- blue pal	a true blue pal
A tongue-twister set	a tongue twister set
A German- Armenian man	a German Armenian man
A sugar-coated woman	a sugar coated woman
A long-stated ancestry	a long stated ancestry

The accurate application or non-use of a hyphen in a modifier can be of crucial significance in making your implication apparent. See the examples listed below:

The earliest known language was *Sanskrit.*

The earliest-known language was *Sanskrit.*

These two sentences do not denote the identical idea at all. The first sentence indicates that, of all the languages we are aware of, *Sanskrit* was the most primitive one to exist (although it was not automatically the earliest one we knew about). The subsequent sentence indicates that, of all the languages, *Sanskrit* was the initial one we knew of (though not inevitably the first one to exist). In fact, the former sentence includes the arrangement [*earliest*] [*known language*], while the following sentence includes the arrangement [*earliest-known*] [*language*]. Once more, these two sentences would be articulated in a different way, although the articulation disparity is mislaid in the lettering; for this reason precise punctuation is crucial if you do not wish to give the wrong impression to your reader completely. If you want your readers to comprehend what you've written punctuation is not an issue of private feel and fancy.

A hyphen can be required by a compound modifier if it appears after the verb. This is a very easy example to follow:

> *His face turned a repulsive dirty-yellow* which is vastly different from: *His face turned a repulsive dirty yellow.*

Conventional practice, particularly in Britain, is in favour of extreme hyphenation, that has given birth to such types as *to-day, co-operate, ski-ing, semi-colon* and even *full-stop;* hyphens like these are futile and unsightly and ought to be kept away from. It is better to write *today, cooperate, skiing, semicolon* and *full stop:* avoid using a hyphen until you feel that it is necessary for the sentence.

At such times prefixes present more problems. While sentences like 'He is reclining on the sofa' are okay, sentences like 'He is reliving his youth' sound slightly strange. It should be written as 're-living' t avoid any confusion about what exactly she is doing. Also words like 're-covered' and 'recovered' can be very different in meaning. It is best to use your own discretion and use whatever seems best. But always try to avoid any confusion. Here are some more examples of hyphens and non-hyphens:

> removed Re-strung
>
> Unionized un-ionised
>
> Premature pre-paid
>
> Antisocial anti-tank

The hyphen is placed only if the word would be tough to interpret without it. As usual, check with a fine lexicon if you're not convinced.

examine, incidentally, that a prefix should not be placed as if it was a distinct word. then all the following examples are incorrect:

post cold war epoch

non capitalist nation

mini bus

anti missile

There are three situations wherein which a hyphen is utterly requisite after a prefix. First, if a capital letter or a digit follows after the hyphen:

non-PC people	un-Aryan races
pre-Renaissance literature	anti-Jew sentiment
post-Holocaust Japan	pre-Raphelite art.

There are also times when a hyphen can be stretched out to encompass three words:

Un-ethical-policy making

pre-dated-computer keyboard.

He is known for his un-reliable-promises during election time.

This is because it would be tough to take in words like predated-computer without a proper break.

Thirdly, if a prefix is placed before a compound word that contains a single gap, the single gap itself should be swapped by a hyphen to avoid the prefixed word from becoming incomprehensible:

Wildlife protection pro-wildlife-protection

Eighteenth century pre-eighteenth-century prose

Vietnam war post-Vietnam-war trauma.

Once again you could really end up confusing your readers if you write words like: * *preeighteenth century prose* or something equally inane. What does preeighteenth mean? What does some century prose have to do with it? As you must have realised this can get terribly confusing. It is much better to just hyphenate the word and say 'pre-eighteenth-century poetry'.

Finally a hyphen can often be used to write pieces of words. To show you some examples:

> The prefix un- can drastically alter the sense of any given statement.
>
> Even under- before a word can alter the meaning.
>
> The suffix –ly is used to turn a word into an adjective often.

Whilst you are writing on the subject of words are you liable to require this use of the hyphen. When you use it, be positive that you have placed the hyphen at the right end of the word you are citing – that is, the point upon which the section has to be allied to another part to construct a word. keep in mind that, when you're writing a suffix, the hyphen must be placed on the identical line as the suffix itself. And you ought not to allocate the hyphen to a position at the end of its line, with the suffix being relegated onto the next line.

There is, nevertheless, one very particular case wherein you may like to write a part of a word in any sort of passage. think about the next instance:

> Pre-war and post-war Vietnam can hardly be recognized as the same place.

There is another way of writing this:

Pre- and post-war Vietnam can hardly be recognized as the same place.

This method is acceptable, but see that the now cut off prefix *pre-* needs a hyphen, because now it is simply a part of a word.

The similar situation arises if you write a part of a word, which is not generally hyphenated, with the aim to steer clear of reiteration:

Nina is opting for socioanalytical and psychoanalytical studies.

This can also be written as:

Nina is opting for socio- and psychoanalytical studies.

The application of the hyphen while writing digits and fractions has been detailed in Chapter 9.

HOW TO USE THE DASH:

A dash (-) is also a horizontal line. But it is longer than a hyphen. For the British usage, if you do not have a dash option on your keyboard, you can use a single hyphen (-) but for the American system, you have to use two hyphens (—). It is better to use double hyphens because it avoids any confusion over whether it is a hyphen or a dash.

The dash has merely one chief use: a pair of dashes can divide a big break from the remainder of the sentence. A big interruption is when the flow of the sentence can be disturbed to a great degree. Notice the word 'pair': in rule, dashes come in pairs. Often, though one of them is omitted. It is the same as the rule for bracketing commas, which set off weak interruptions. These are some instances:

The most intelligent man – if there is indeed such a category – would also need to exercise his brains to retain them.

The Vietnam War – even excluding the aftermath – was perhaps one of the most destructive wars.

When I went to see China – as part of the world tour I was taking – I was dumbfounded at seeing the Great Wall of China.

Sometimes a break can come just once, when the interruption is just one. Then a single dash is used:

I thought she lived here – didn't she?

Robert saw the famous temples of India in 1956 – they are quite different now.

Did you see the match – or not?

Remember that the dash is used to represent a break. It is therefore technically incorrect to say things like:

Did he come here – anyway, I don't really want to know.

These sorts of sentences are frequently used in short story or novel writing. They can add a bit of variety to the sentence structure. And they can portray character a bit more, but avoid using them in any other way.

Also sometimes it can happen that a sentence is broken off unexpectedly without being concluded, then we can again use a single dash:

These are often quoted to be the most famous last words, "Look ma, no hand-"

As you will realize, the dash here is placed directly after the word, with no gap to separate them. This goes to show that the word was not completed when it was broken off. This dash indicates a breakage of the words that were being used prior to an abrupt end. It is different from ellipses which go to show that a sentence has trailed off into silence. This is explained in greater details in Chapter 8.

In this fashion when a dash separates two lines, make sure that it is placed at the end of the first line and not at the beginning of the second line. This is something that people often either totally ignore or don't consider important enough. But it goes a long way in making your composition look neat, educated and appealing.

Remember that the dash can also be used while representing numerical and various other ranges. For example:

> A – Z: This means that all the alphabets (from A to Z) are included in whatever is being talked about.
>
> Fat content in most meals is 2% – 8%.
>
> The Jaipur – Delhi train has been delayed for two hours.
>
> The great Indian freedom fighter, Bhagat Singh, lived from 1907 – 31.
>
> Russia wished to start a Trans – Atlantic train so that travel to turkey would have been made easier.

However, if you do not wish to use a dash you can always replace it with a 'to'. For example:

> The Jaipur to Delhi train has been delayed for two hours.
>
> Fat content in most meals is from 2% to 8%.

But remember not to use between in such sentences. For example:

> The fat content in most meals is between 2% to 8%.

Between cannot be used in this style. Even the third sentence can be written in a better style. The example I have shown you is largely informal. It is better to write dates in full digit form. For example:

> The great Indian freedom fighter, Bhagat Singh, lived from 1907 to 1931.

These are all the ways to use a dash. But because you now know all the ways to use a dash you should not hurriedly place it in all sorts of ways in your compositions. Use it as sparingly as possible. If overused, the dash can give your writing an incoherent, rambling and winded out look. Also avoid using the dash for any function apart from a wish to set off a big pause or marking a variety. But keep in mind that the dash can never be used in stead of a hyphen, after a colon or after a heading. It cannot be used to introduce a direct reference, excluding occasional usage of this type in novels, but do try and keep it as minimum as possible.

There is one final note to be made. Though it is very minor. In a particular method of writing, which is now thought to be conservative and refined, the extra-long dash is intermittently used to stand for the exclusion of some alphabets from a word or a name. As an example we can see some of the books by many Victorian novelists who often wrote *d—l* in place of *devil,* and even *be d-d!* as an alternative for *be damned!* Such a style of writing is now considered very amusing and gives a fuddy-duddy approach. Nowadays milder oaths and swears are often written and more the stronger ones have asterisks (*) placed in the middle. Often authors did not want to give their narratives any specific location. Then they would write things like 'She lived in M –', or 'he was in the -regiment.' Since novels are now vying for authentication appeal this sort of usage is now no longer in vogue.

CHAPTER 7

A BIT ABOUT QUOTATION MARKS

QUOTATION MARKS AND DIRECT QUOTATIONS:

The sentences that start with inverted commas, which implies commas placed on the top of the words are known as Quotation marks. There are tow types of quotes: single quotes (') and double quotes (" "). The use of quotation marks, also called inverted commas, is very slightly complicated by the fact that there are two types: single quotes (' ') and double quotes (" ").

The usage of these quotes differs from country to country according to their rules like in Britain they normally use single quotes even in South Africa this rule is followed, but in the countries like America, Canada, Australia, and New Zealand they prefer the use of double quotes. Although you will find certain advantages in the use of Double quotes, its use is helpful for those who are working with publication houses and print media. The reader due to light ink mark can overlook the printed single quotes, whereas the double quotes look more prominent on the printed material and can be read conveniently by any reader.

The main use of quotation marks is to understand the direct dialogue easily that is denoted by a pair of quotation marks, which is used to enclose a Direct Quotation. For example:

> Mr. John Grisham eminently exclaimed, 'Ich bin ein Berliner!'
>
> President Bush is quite fond of declaring, 'I'm not ashamed of anything.'
>
> 'The only emperor,' writes Sir Sean Conroy, 'is the emperor of ice cream.'

In these examples you will find that the sentences that are enclosed in quotes are the spoken words of the person who is being mentioned as the speaker. The part, which is not spoken, but mentions about the person who is the speaker of those dialogues is always placed outside the quotes, even if, as in the last example, this means using two sets of quotes because the quotation has been interrupted. (The commas in the last example set off a weak interruption, as usual; their presence has nothing to do with the quotation.) You should have noticed an extraordinary thing where: the first comma in the last example comes *inside* the quotes, even though it is not part of the quotation. It dose not have any importance rather it opposes the general principle of the Punctuation, but these days this illogical style has become common in the language. According to basic rules I recommend to use the Comma outside the quotes as it is mentioned below:

> 'The only emperor', writes Sir Sean Conroy, 'is the emperor of ice cream.'

But, many people do not accept this and sometimes they may confront you. If you want to know more about this topic go ahead.

Otherwise, on the other hand you should not put quotes around anything other than a word-for-word quotation. The following example, for instance, is wrong:

> Jet Lee declared that 'Genius was one per cent inspiration and ninety-nine per cent perspiration.'

This example does not clarify, that whether Thomas Jet Lee reproduced the quoted words, so there are three ways to correct the sentence. First is to drop the quotes like:

> Jet Lee declared that genius was one per cent inspiration and ninety-nine per cent perspiration.

In the second way, rewrite the sentence, by using the exact dialogue of Jet Lee:

> According to Jet Lee, 'Genius is one per cent inspiration and ninety-nine per cent perspiration.'

The third way is, to move the quotes so that they enclose only Lee's exact words:

> Jet Lee declared that genius was 'one per cent inspiration and ninety-nine per cent perspiration'.

These three examples are prefect where the Lee's exact words are enclosed in the quotes.

Remember that a Quotation is only started with Quotation marks

The sentence, which has Quotation, should be punctuated with the normal rule apart from the addition of the quotation marks. Do not put unnecessary punctuation marks into the sentence just to warn the reader that a quotation is coming up: that's what the quotation marks are for. Here are some common mistakes:

> The leader stated: 'I am not a crook.'
>
> The Leader stated:– 'I am not a crook.'

In the first example the colon before starting the quotation is absolutely senseless, while the surprising group of punctuation in the second is grotesque. (Also remember, that a colon can never be followed by a hyphen or a dash.) The correct style, which is recommend as follows:

> The Leader stated 'I am not a crook.'

By inserting more dots and scribbles to this absolutely clear sentence would not do anything to improve it. Do not use unnecessary marks punctuation marks in any sentence.

On the other hand, very many people prefer to use a comma before an opening quote, as follows:

> The Leader stated, 'I am not a crook.'

The careful user finds such commas to be unnecessary, since they do no work at all, but most publishers insist upon them. But those who are working with publications, then, they will perhaps find themselves appreciated by using them.

However, the presence of quotation marks does not eliminate the requirement for using other punctuations that are necessary for the sentence.

For example:

> According to Jet Lee, 'Genius is one per cent inspiration and ninety-nine per cent perspiration.'
>
> 'The only emperor,' writes Sir Sean Conroy, 'is the emperor of ice cream.'

In these examples bracketing commas are used, in the beginning of the fragile interruptions, which has no connection with the presence of a quotation, which is it suitably manifested by the quotation marks.

Here is another example:

> Julia Moore had one fair rule for handling men: 'Tell the attractive ones they're stylish, and tell the stylish ones they're attractive.'

In this example the colon is not being used for the quotation, which follows. Rather, it is placed to introduce an explanation of what comes before the colon. There it is just a chance that the colon is placed before the quotation.

This last example demonstrates another point, which is about quotations: the quotation inside the quote marks starts with a capital letter if it is a complete sentence, but not otherwise. Let us look once again at two versions of the Jet Lee sentence:

> According to Jet Lee, 'Genius is one per cent inspiration and ninety-nine per cent perspiration.'
>
> Jet Lee declared that genius was 'one per cent inspiration and ninety-nine per cent perspiration'.

The first quotation is a complete sentence and therefore it starts with an initial capital letter; the second is not a complete sentence and so receives no capital.

There is a situation where the use of single quotes in the place of double quotes can be somewhat an irrelevant. This is when the quotation contains an apostrophe, especially near the end, like in this sentence:

> The renowned Scholar Cavendish concludes that 'The Turks' pressure on the Balkans has been more continuing than the Greeks' ever was.'

While an apostrophe is usually identical from a closing quote mark, the reader may be temporarily misinformed by thinking that the person has come to the end of the quotation when he has not. That is the reason why I suggest using double quotes:

> The renowned Scholar Cavendish concludes, "The Turks' pressure on the Balkans has been more continuing than the Greeks' ever was."

The problem goes away with double quotes.

Things can get complex when you mention a quotation that already consist another quotation within it. In this rare condition, the rule is to begin the internal quotation with the *other* type of quotation marks. So, if you're using double quotes:

> The employment News agency declared, "In the survey to find out the unemployment records as 'unsatisfactory' is an abuse to the government."

Here if you're using single quotes:

> The employment News agency declared, 'In the survey to find out the unemployment records as "unsatisfactory" is an abuse to the government.'

Logically, here if you have a quotation inside a quotation than you should rewrite the whole sentence. Otherwise, you will just mislead your reader in the tangle of quotation marks.

Suppose one has a long quotation that you want to exhibit indented in the middle of the page, there is no need to place quotes around it, however you should be confident that one recognize it clearly as a quotation in your main text. Here is an example cited from G. V. Carey's famous book on punctuation, *Mind the Stop* (Carey 1958):

> Where he has designed the punctuation as being governed two-thirds by rule and one-third by personal conviction. He attempted by not emphasizing the former to the elimination of the latter, but he suggested not knuckling

> under to those who actually claim for themselves absolute freedom to do what they please in the matter.

There is nothing wrong to enclose this passage in quotes, but there is no need, where he referred as noticeably recognized it as a quotation, which is exactly what quotation marks usually do. No punctuation should be used where it does not play any function.

Sometimes it is necessary to break up a quotation that is mentioned in order to clarify something. To do this you can enclose your explanation in square brackets (never parentheses). Suppose I want to mention a famous passage from the eighteenth-century German writer Adolph Hitler:

> I want my nation [Germany] appear set to sway the destinies of half the globe.

The passage from which this sentence is taken had previously clarified which two nations the author was talking about. My quotation, however, does not make this clear, and so I have introduced the necessary information enclosed in square brackets.

Many authors have a habit of inserting their own initials within the square brackets, preceded by a dash. Thus, that example might have looked like this:

> I want my nation [Germany] appear set to sway the destinies of half the globe.

This is not wrong, there is no necessity to do that, because the square brackets already make it clear it's meaning.

You should be familiar with particular interruption. It occurs when the passage you are quoting has some kind of mistake, which you have to fix it for your reader since the mistake exists in the original passage, and has not been introduced by you. For the clarification, you have to use the Latin word sic enclosed in the square bracket, which means 'thus', directly following the mistake. For any kind of mistakes like: a spelling mistake, a grammatical error, the use of the wrong word, or wrong a statement. Here are some examples, which are meant to be direct quotations:

> We have not receieved [*sic*] your letter.
>
> The number of students are [*sic*] larger than usual.
>
> The All Blacks won the match with a fortuitous [*sic*] try in the final minute.
>
> The last mammoth died about 70,000 years ago [*sic*].

(The word *receieved* is misspelled; the form *are* has been used where *is* is required; the word *fortuitous,* which means 'accidental', has been used where *fortunate* was intended; the last statement is grotesquely false.) Note the word sic is usually italicized, if italics are available. Also remember that sic is not used simply to emphasize part of a quotation: it is used only to draw attention to an error.

Suppose you want to highlight part of a quotation, than you can do it by italicizing that portion. Here is a sentence quoted from Steven Pinker's book *The Language Instinct:*

> Many suggested rules of grammar are *just too stupid* and should be deleted from the usage handbooks [emphasis added].

In the above sentence, the square brackets shows that the italics were not present in the original but that is added there, in order to draw attention on that part of the quotation. In Chapter 8 we shall consider the further use of italics.

Sometimes, from a quotation words can be deleted or added on. If you wish to add the prevailing bits, you can do this by inserting an ellipsis (. . .) (also called a suspension or omission marks) to represent a missing section of a quotation. In a condition where, you need to provide one or two extra words to link up the pieces of the quotation, you put those extra words in square brackets to show that they are not part of the quotation. An instance is where you need to change a small letter to a capital letter, then put that capital letter inside square brackets.

Peter Gately was struck with paralysis from the neck downwards, and . . . he was terribly misdiagnosed as emotionally retarded when he unsuccessfully tried to learn how to speak . . . he was raised by a loving family . . . [but] only when he was thirty-one did a disbelieving doctor . . . prescribe for him an examination aid. Able to hear speech at last, he began learning English.

Be careful while using an ellipsis, it should not misrepresent the sense of the original passage.

Finally, there only remains confusion about inserting the other punctuation marks inside or outside the quotation marks. There are basically two opinions on this issue, which are: the *logical view* and the *conventional view.* American usage sticks closely to the conventional view; British usage prefers the logical view, but, here also you find an exception.

The logical view states that the only punctuation marks, which should be placed inside the quotation marks are those that figure as the part of the quotation, while others should be placed outside. The conventional view, in contrast, lays emphasis on the placement of the most other punctuation marks inside a closing quote, regardless of whether they form part of the quotation. For Example

> "The only thing we have to fear", said Mr. Roosevelt, "is fear itself."
>
> Ballinger never said "Accent is predictable"; he said "Accent is predictable – if you're a mind-reader."

The Scientist condemned what he called, "band-aid solutions".

And here they are punctuated according to the conventional view:

"The only thing we have to fear," said Mr. Roosevelt, "is fear itself."

The Linguists never said, "Accent is predictable;" he said, "Accent is predictable – if you're a mind-reader."

The Scientist condemned what he called, "band-aid solutions."

Note the placements of the punctuations in the examples such as: the comma after fear in the first example,

The semicolon can be *predictable* in the second, and the final full stop in the third. Since they are not part of the quotations, and so the logical view places them outside the quote marks, whereas the conventional view places them inside, on the theory that a closing quote should always follow another punctuation mark.

In this case the careful user of the language prefer to use the Logical View., I would simply advise you to stick to this view. However, it is a fact that American usage sticks severely to the conventional view, and you may find it challenging to convince an American publisher to desist from changing your logical punctuation. In comparison the British usage, usually prefers the logical view, but with one contradictory and peculiar exception: British publishers usually emphasise on putting a comma inside closing quotes, even when it logically belongs outside. So a British publisher will usually insist on the conventional style with the Roosevelt example mentioned as above, but on the logical style with the other two, which is unexplained.

> The freedom fighter Lokmanya Tilak's newspaper *Kesari* contains the line, which evoked the whole nation, " Give me your blood and I will give you freedom."

It is correct. Let us attempt it with conventional punctuation, as chosen in the USA:

> The freedom fighter Lokmanya Tilak's newspaper *Kesari* contains the line, which evoked the whole nation, " Give me your blood and I will give you freedom"

This is absolutely incorrect, since the line in question is only the first of two lines making up a complete sentence, and therefore does not end in a full stop, as it seems that recommended by the conventional punctuation:

> Give me your blood and I will give you freedom

Here if we take up the example that we quoted in Chapter 6 then we shall see the perils of following the rules sometimes:

> These are often quoted as the most famous last words, "Look ma, no hand-".

In this example if you put the full stop inside the closing quotes, as needed by the conventionalists, which would construct an senseless sentence, since the whole point of the quotation is that the lamented man didn't live long enough to finish it.

Your preference can be followed in this kind of sentences on the condition that it should make sense. Suppose you have you chosen to follow logical punctuation, where you will have the feeling of containment, but you should be ready to face the contradictory remarks from the opposition.

HOW TO USE SCARE QUOTES:

The use of quotation marks can be comprehended to cases where there no direct quotation. Here is an example:

> Linguists sometimes use a method they call 'inverted reconstruction'.

The phrase in quote marks is not a quotation from anyone in particular, but only a term, which does some people – in this case, linguists, use. In this instance what the writer is doing here is *distancing* him from the term in quotes. That is, he's stating, 'Look, that's what they call it. I'm not responsible for this term.' In this situation, there is no suggestion that the writer rejects the phrase in quotes, but very frequentlys there *is* a suggestion of disapproval:

The Institute for Personal Knowledge has introduced a course in 'self-awareness exercises'.

In the repetition, the writer's quotes mean 'this is *their* term, not mine', but this time there is definitely a hint of a sneer: the writer is implying that, while the Institute may *call* their course 'self-awareness exercises', but in reality they are making money by boasting.

This usage of Quotation marks is informally called scare quotes. Scare quotes are quotation marks placed around a word or phrase that helps the writer to create a distance where there is the chance of any contradictions.

The case where it give the impression of the informal context, so that the reader regard it as unfamiliar or mysterious; perhaps they consider it to be inaccurate or misleading, or wrong impression. Generally scare quotes are used to express irony or sarcasm:

> The Titanic is drowning into the 'safe haven' of Ocean

The point here is that the town has been officially declared a safe haven by the UN, whereas in fact, as the quote marks make clear, it is anything but safe. Here's another example:

> Nassirudin Shah made dozens of Hollywood movies before getting the 'lead role' in 'The League Of Extraordinary Gentleman.'

The phrase 'lead role' is the industry's conventional label for main role, and here the writer is showing that she recognizes this phrase as nothing more than a false euphemism.

It is essential to realize the isolated result of scare quotes. Here the Quotation marks are not appropriately used simply with the intention of draw attention to words, and all those pubs which declare *We Sell 'usual sea Food'* are unintentionally suggesting to a educate reader that they are indeed serving up microwaved dishes.s

Some writers possibly take the use of scare quotes extensively.:

> He is so 'worked up' with his employees these days.

In this example the writer made a strange use by using the phrase 'worked up', but it also represents the distaste for the phrase by covering it in quotes. Possibly it is represented in the slang, which is American style. The use of scare quotes in this way is the orthographic equivalent of holding the phrase at arm's length with one hand and pinching your nose with the other.

It is not recommended to use the Scare Quotes in this manner, but even then you want to use it try to avoid using quotes unless you particularly want to be ironic. Concurrent usage a word and viewing that you don't approve of it will only make you sound like an old-fashioned person.

THE USE OF QUOTATION MARKS IN TITLES:

In the yesteryears, there was the practice to enclose all titles in quotation marks: titles of books, titles of poems, titles of films, titles of newspapers, and so on. These days this usage has been disappeared, and a new style, which has come up, is to write most titles in italics, that are explained in the Chapter 8, at least in the scholastic scenario,, it is still common to enclose the titles of articles in journals and magazines in quotes, in addition to the titles of chapters in books – therefore here is the reference of a article 'Punctuation and human freedom'.

In British usage, still, they normally use single quotes for this purpose, while in American usage usually prefers double quotes here too.

There is nothing wrong while referring to a newspaper as 'The Guardian', or to a book as 'Uncle Sam's room', but these days it is considered, as out of fashion, so it is better to use italics rather than quotation marks, unless it is written by hand.

LET'S TALK ABOUT WORDS:

There is a special use of quotation marks that is quotation marks are used when we are talking about words. The extraordinary utilization of all varieties of English language usually use only single quotes, and not double quotes (though some Americans use double quotes even here). (This is another advantage of using double quotes for ordinary purposes, since this special use can then be easily distinguished.) Consider the following examples:

Males are physically stronger than females.

'Males' is an irregular plural.

In the first example the word 'males' is used in the ordinary way, which refers to male human beings. In the second, however, we are doing something exceptionally different: where there is no reference of human being, but instead it refers to the word 'males'. By placing quotes around the word for making the sense clear. It is required when you are particularly writing about the language.

If you are unnecessarily getting confused, so a look at a sample:

> An archetypal youthful speaker in reading has done, not did, and frequently also does for do and dos for does.

It is a whole lot easier to read with some suitable quotation marks:

> A distinctive immature speaker in reading has 'done', not 'did', and regularly also 'does' for 'do' and 'dos' for 'does'.

If you fail to craft this useful orthographic distinction can, in extraordinary cases, which lead to illogicality:

> The use of word processor came about 1910.

Suppose the succeeding meaning, a writing the first will create temporary disorder in the reader's mind. (The next statement is true; the first is incorrect by about seventy years.) There is a predominantly clear example of the way in which good punctuation works: in speech, the phrases *the word processor* and *the word 'processor'* sound fairly unlike, since they are emphasized differently in writing, the stress difference is missing, and punctuation should step in to do the job.

Printed books regularly use italics for showing words, rather than using the quotation marks quotation marks. Suppose you are using a keyboard, which can produce italics, you can use italics in this way, and certainly this practice is preferable to the use of quotes. Look at the Chapter 9 for more details.

In a condition, although, italics are not achievable: while providing concise translations (or *glosses,* as they are called) of the foreign words. Here's an example:

> The word in English language 'Exist' is resulting from the Latin word in esse. that has the literal meaning 'in being'.

The illustration represents the typical means of describing foreign words: these foreign word are shown into italics, plus an English translation, which is given that follows in single quotes, by no other punctuation. Scrutinize with the intention of not using a comma or something else separates the foreign word from the annotation.

It can be done with the English words either:

> Words like *stationary* 'not moving' and *stationery* 'writing materials' should be cautiously represented
>
> In this case, it is clearly necessary to use italics for citing English words, reserving the single quotes for the glosses.

The Summary of quotation marks:

- place quotation marks (single or double) enclosed the precise words of a direct quotation.
- in a quotation, use a postponement to mark removed matter and square brackets to highlight added material.
- to keep space from a word or phrase, that his used ironically, so use quotation marks.
- a word or phrase , that spoken about something should be enclosed by quotation marks.

CHAPTER 8

THE OTHER USAGE OF SYMBOLS IN THE ENGLISH LANGUAGE

HOW TO USE ITALICS:

The italics can be produced by any word processors, they are displayed – *like these.* If you can't produce italics, the conservative alternative is to use underlining in the case of not having the facility of changing in the italics– like this. There are many uses of italics.

The italics are generally used for emphasis or contrast – which is, to draw attention to some specific part of a copy. For example:

> The Battle of France was fought in March 18 1 5, three weeks *after* the peace treaty had been signed.
>
> The renowned linguist Peter John says, 'Many regulatory convention of grammar are *just plain dumb* and should be removed from the usage handbooks' [emphasis added].
>
> The customary use of English grammar requires 'insensitive' relative than '*unsensitive*'.
>
> Lemmings have, not one, but *three* kinds of sex genes.

The first two illustrations are insisting and the last two illustrate the contrast. This is the typical method of describing the emphasis or contrast; here one should try to avoid the use quotation marks or other punctuation marks for this reason.

There is another explanation of using the italics, which is as explained in Chapter 7, is to show titles of complete works: books, films, journals, musical compositions, etc.:

> We watched a performance of the *Kenny G* on Saturday.
>
> The book which is written by Chomsky *Syntactic Structures* has revolutionized linguistics.
>
> Mel Gibson won his Oscar for his memorable performance in the movie *Braveheart.*
>
> There is an exception: the names of holy books are regularly *not* written in italics. So, the (Holy) Bible and the (Holy) Koran, are not written in italics.

Note, conversely, when a name, which is only a conventional description, is also not shown in the italics:

> Beethovon's ninth symphony is commonly known as the *New World* symphony.

In this example, the label 'Beethovon's ninth symphony' is not strictly a title, and hence is not italicized.

The another use of italics is done for foreign words while talking about them. Examples:

> The French word *pathétique is* usually best translated as 'moving', not as 'pathetic'.
>
> The German word *Gemütlichkeit is* not easy to translate into English.
>
> The Sicilian tradition *of omertà* has long protected the Mafia.

At Basque festivals, a favourite entertainment is the *sokamuturra,* in which people run in front of a bull which is restricted by ropes controlled by handlers.

Here the use of italics while using the foreign words and phrases which are not included in the assimilated English language.

Psychologists are interested in the phenomenon of *déjà vu*.

This analysis is not in accord with the *Sprachgefühl* of native speakers.

One should refer to a dictionary in the case of unconfirmed words and phrases.

As mentioned in Chapter 7, the another use of italics is done displaying the English words , which are being talked about, as an alternative to single quotes:

It is not known from where the word lad has been derived.

Note when there is the difference between *premier* (an adjective meaning 'first' or 'most important') and *premiere* (a noun meaning 'first performance').

In conclusion, the italics have been used in definite disciplines for diverse detailed causes. The most common ones are:. In biology, genus and species names of living creatures are italicized:

The earliest known member of the genus *Homo is H. habilis.*

The cedar waxwing *(Bombycilla cedrorum) is* a familiar American bird.

Note that a type name always has a capital letter, while a species name never does.

Second, names of lawful cases are italicized:

> The famous case of *Brown v. Board of Education* was a landmark in American legal history.

In this instance, the abbreviation *v.*, which stands for *versus* ('against') stands in roman type, not in italics. Note also that the American abbreviation is *vs.*:

> A famous case of *S.R.Bommai vs.Indian Government for the argument of the Article 356* was a landmark in Indian Parliament.

> Special note: When a sentence has been containing a phrase which is usually included in the italics and an instance where for some reason the entire sentence required to be italicized, there the phrase that would usually be in italics goes into normal roman type in its place. So, if for some

cause the last example sentence needs to be italicized, the result would look like this:

> The famous case of *S.R.Bommai vs.Indian Government for the argument of the Article 356* was a landmark in Indian Parliament.

THE USE OF BOLDFACE:

When the impression of the Boldface letters displayed the extra-black ones – like these, which can be obtained from the word processors. They are used in few instances for using it.

Firstly, they are used for mentioning the chapter titles and section headings, accurately, which is practiced in the book.

Secondly, they are used for mentioning the captions to illustrations, tables and graphs.

Thirdly, they are sometimes where it is used to give very strong emphasis, as an alternative to italics. In this book, I have used them in this method very regularly – probably too commonly:

A colon is never followed by a hyphen or a dash.

Finally, the boldface is used frequently to introduce significant new expressions.

This book is the ideal example of all the use of the boldface: the name of each new punctuation mark is introduced in boldface.

The sensible use of boldface can offer diversity and create a page more eye-catching, but it is not at all necessary. When you cannot produce boldface, then there is the option of using the ordinary roman type for chapter and section headings and captions, also one can use italics for emphasis and important terms. When the boldface is used, don't overdo it.

WHERE TO PUT SMALL ALPHABETS:

This is exactly like its literal meaning, so it's known as small capitals : THEY LOOK LIKE THIS. They are used a universal use: certain abbreviations are commonly written in small capitals. In particular, the abbreviations BC and AD are frequently so printed:

The time of the origin of Jainism and Buddhism is recorded in the history from 6th century B.C.

The age of the Mauryan Era started after 350 A.D.

Remember that the American usage prefers to write the time of day with small capitals:

(A) The earthquake struck at 6:40 AM.

On the contrary in the British usage, this would emerge as follows:

The earthquake struck at 6.40 a.m.

There is a new fashion, which is practiced by some publishers these days that is putting *all* abbreviations in small capitals, but it should not be copied.

The word processors can produce small capitals; when you can't produce them, use full capitals instead:

> The age of the Mauryan Era started after 350 A.D..

There is the seldom use of , small capitals such as to emphasis, but it is generally suggested to use italics for this, or even boldface.

THE USE OF PARENTHESES:

Parentheses (( )), are also called round brackets, they usually occurs in the .group. They are used generally for one major use and one or two minor uses.

Most frequently, a pair of parentheses to display a strong or weak interruption, rather like a pair of dashes or a pair of bracketing commas. When there is a instances of strong interruption, it is very frequently appeared with either dashes or parentheses:

> The Bomb shelling on the Heroshima – and there is no doubt that the destruction was deliberate – horrified the world.
>
> The Bomb shelling on the Heroshima (and there is no doubt that the destruction was deliberate) horrified the world.

On contrary, as a rule the use of parentheses suggested, rather than dashes or bracketing commas, when the disruption is best regarded as a type of 'aside' from the writer to the reader:

On the (rare!) occasion when you use a Latin abbreviation, be sure to punctuate it correctly.

The mutiny of the Bounty (as you may recall from your school days) put an end to Rome's conquest of Islands.

The Basque language is not (as the old legend has it) exceedingly difficult to learn.

The of use parentheses to begin an interruption which only gives the additional information or a concise clarification of an unknown expression:

The number of living languages (currently about *6000,* by most estimates) is decreasing rapidly.

The *bodegas* (wine cellars) of the Rica are an essential stop on any visit to northern Spain.

The royal portraits of Velázquez (or Velásquez) are justly renowned.

In the above mentioned two examples, where the phrases in parentheses simply give an optional spelling of the painter's name and the birth and death dates of the philosopher. In the above cited examples, neither dashes nor bracketing commas would be achievable, apart from, that you might have the little possibility to use dashes in the first. Note the method , which has been followed for the introduction of new punctuation mark in this book.

The whole sentence can be put into parentheses, or even a sequence of sentences, if they represent a disruption of an suitable kind:

> The survey states that 35% of girls aged *16-18* smoke frequently, but that only *25%* of boys in this age bracket do so. (These figures are provided by a recent newspaper survey.)

Note a sentence in parentheses is capitalized and punctuated in the standard method.

Never repeat parentheses for the sake of filling the entire sentence inside another:

> The first-ever international cricket match (very few cricket fans are aware of this) was played between Canada and the United States in *1857*

These kinds of sentences are practices by the person who neither plan their sentences nor correct their sentences afterwards. Suppose you found that you have done it, and then rewrite the sentences in the better manner:

> Very few cricket fans are aware that the first-ever international cricket match was played between Canada and the United States in *1857*. Or
>
> The first-ever international cricket match was played between Canada and the United States in 1857. Very few cricket fans are aware of this.

The Parentheses can also be used to represent options like:

> The referees who decide whether an abstract should be accepted will not know the name(s) of the author(s).
>
> The (French) horn is an extraordinarily complicated instrument to play.

The point of the last example is that the names *french horn* and *horn* denote the same instrument.

To conclude, parentheses are used to enclose numbers or letters in a detailed integrated in the body of a text:

> A book offer arranged for a potential publisher should comprise at least (1) an explanation of the content.
>
> (2) a classification of the intended circulation.
>
> (3) a clarification of the necessity of evaluating a book.

(4) an evaluation with any challenging books previously available in the market.

To view , in the comparison, the marks like dashes and bracketing commas, you should always write both parentheses:

> He was smitten by a *coup de foudre* (as the French none too romantically put it).

Sometimes you found that you are placed a set of parentheses inside another. At times it can be avoided, but always try to avoid because it makes the sentence difficult to understand.

The ways to use Square Brackets:

The only one commonly used square brackets ([ ]), Which is mentioned in the chapter 7 was . It is used to begin a break with a direct quotation; go through to that chapter for more instructions.

The square brackets are used in rare cases just for citing references; it is mentioned in the Chapter 9.

In the professional and technical subjects like mathematics and linguistics employ square brackets for some particular reasons of their own, which cannot be mentioned in this topic.

THE PLACES WHERE YOU CAN USE THE ELLIPSIS:

The ellipsis (. . .), Which is also known as the suspension or omission marks, generally has two uses.

1.The ellipsis is used to display the matter that has been removed from the omitted from the middle of a direct quotation; in the chapter 8 this topic has been dealt with further explanations.

2. The ellipsis is also used where the sentence is not finished. It is not like hyphen, that is used for displaying a sudden break come

in a word, !), the postponement represents that the writer or speaker has intentionally took a break in a word by putting a pause in it.:

New Jersey gets a major earthquake about every fifty years.
There are ninety years since the last one . . .

The second style is more representative in the journalistic style than in the official writing; there is a exception in the case where you are citing a direct quotation that is needed there, but try to avoid the use of the ellipsis in the formal context.

THE USE OF A SLASH:

The slash (/), also known as the oblique, the virgule, the stroke, the solidus or the shilling mark, it has various trivial uses.

1.The slash is used to divide the given options:

The students must possess a good university degree in Spanish and/or have worked for two years in a country where the Spanish is the official language.

Suppose the work of a writer is bad, the reader may quickly decide that s/he has better things to do.

The examples are not comfortable while visualizing them so try to write the options in the full words:

Each candidate must carry his or her identity card.

Such method is very common in the job advertisements:

The University of Saffron Walden wishes to appoint a lecturer/senior lecturer in media studies.

2.The slash can be used to show a period of time.:

The 1979/80 football season was marred by frequent scandals.

This office is open Tuesday/ Saturday each week.

3. It is also used to display the word *per* in units, which is particularly used in the scientific context:

The density of iron is 7.87 g/cm'.

Light travels at 300,000 km/sec.

4. The slash is used for displaying fractions, like in 2\3 or 3\2; this also called the scratch. (Look at the next section for usage.)

5. For writing some abbreviations the slash is used, but practically you will find it in very rare contexts like *c/o* for 'care of in addresses:

My postal address is Dina John, c/o Samuel Hayward, 22 The Palma, Oaks, New Jersy NJ 17 4GH.

6. In a poem or prose the slash is employed for dividing the lines of poetry when a poem is written firmly or not written in the pattern of line by line.:

When you have reached in the climax of your life /And nodding by the fire, take down this book/And slowly read of the soft look/Your eyes had once, and of their shadows deep. (John donne)

THE STYLES OF WRITING THE NUMERALS, FRACTIONS AND DATES:

The complex digits from twenty-one to ninety-nine, when these numerals are written in the words there you put hyphens:

The Office is divided into sixty-four different sections.

Sam was only thirty-five years old when he died.

Do not put additional hyphens for the bigger units.

The year, which has three hundred and sixty-six days, is called the Leap year.

The highest score with three darts is one hundred and eighty.

The units or the digits are always are written in words in the formal context.

The French flag has three stripes.

They have four candidates for president.

Never write in this form:

- The French flag has 3 stripes.
- They have 4 candidates for president.

In the case of bigger units, there you have choice to write in the digits.:

The explosion killed 50 people and 230 people were severely injured.

The archeological department found the evidence of the town that existed 5000 years ago.

On the other hand it very common to write the units up to ninety-nine, and actually a few publications are recommending for using this style.

The explosion killed thirty-seven people and over 200 people were severely injured.

There are different styles a four digits unit other than the dates like in the American style, they don't use comma and in the British style they use the comma. Therefore Americans write 5000 *years* and 2700 *people,* while Britons often write 5,000 *years* and 2,700 *people.*

A is not recommended to use that, but it depends on the perceptions of an individuals. A five-digit or larger digit always takes one or more commas: 67,000 *refugees,* 240,000 *cases of AIDS,* 3,560,453 *patents.*

Obviously, if want to make an exception for addresses and other unusual instances, in which digits are always written with units:

The Prime Minister lived for years at 4 Howitt Road in Belsize Park.

Remember that never start any sentence with a unit., since it is considered a wrong manner,: But if cannot avoid it than write in the words:

- 556 MPs sit in Parliament.
- Five hundred and fifty six MPs sit in Parliament.
- There are 650 MPs in Parliament.

The fractions are always written with hyphens:

Almost three-fourths of the earth's surface is water. More than one-half of babies born are male.

Look at the following examples

My mind is divided in a dilemma, where one half is telling me to do it and one half is stopping me to do that. .

Here the phrase *one half is* not really a fraction at all.

So in the formal context, a fraction is always written out. Never write it like this:

- About 3/4 of the earth's surface is water.

For mentioning a date you can use commas, this method is very common these days, but other way of writing a date is like:

It was on 22 April 1976 that Jane Eyre was released

On December 8, 1933, the Germany attacked Russia.

She died on the last day of November 1983.

The earlier style is also written by putting commas in like:

It was on 18 April, 1775, that Paul Revere made his famous ride.

On December 7, 1941, the Japanese attacked Pearl Harbor.

She died on the last day of November, *1843.*

Use any style as long as you are constant.

Important note: The format of the British of writing a date is like day-month-year, whereas in the American style it is like month-day-year. Therefore, British write 21 *March,* while Americans write *March* 21. So one has to remember their style while corresponding in these countries in the Briton, 2/7/87 means 17 July, 1964, while to an American it means *May* 6, 1974. The safer side to avoid these contradictions is to mention the date in full while corresponding with these countries.

HOW TO USE DIACRITICS:

Diacritics, informally it is known as 'accents', which are the small little dots and squiggles which, in many languages that are represented above, below or on top of certain letters of the alphabet to signify something about their accent. Thus, French has words like *été* 'summer', *août* 'August', *ça* 'that' and *père* 'father'; German has *Wörter* 'words' and *tschüss* 'good-bye'; Spanish has *mañana* 'tomorrow' and *angel* 'angel'; Norwegian has *bred* 'bread' and *frå* 'from'; Polish has ³*za* 'tear', Ÿ*le* 'badly' and piec 'five'; Turkish has *ku*° 'bird' and göz 'eye'; Welsh has *ty* 'house' and *sïo* 'hiss', and so on. When you represent a word, a name or a passage from a foreign language by using diacritics, the attempt should be made to reproduce those diacritics sincerely. The most word processors can produce at least the common diacritics.

You require to cite the names of the person, place or titles of literature or the musical terms . The French politician is *François Mitterrand,* the Spanish golfer *is Jose-Maria Olazábal,* the Polish linguist is *Jerzy Kury³owicz,* the Turkish national hero is *Mustafa Kemal Atatürk,* the town in the former Yugoslavia is *Gora•de,* Wagner's opera is the *Götterdämmerung* and the French film is *Zazie dans le Métro.* So far as you can produce them, therefore, these are the forms you should use even when writing in English. But don't overdo it. If an accepted English form exists, use that: write *Munich,* not *München, Montreal,* not *Montréal, The Magic Flute,* not *Die Zauberflöte.*

In the English language, diacritics do not usually applied, but there are three situations where they can be applied:

1.The foreign words and phrases, which are included in the English language, where as some of them are not commonly accepted in the language. Such terms should be written with their original diacritics, and they can also be represented in the italics, try to mention about its foreign origin.:

Lloyd George was the Tories' *bête noire.*

She was an artist *manquée.*

The *Wörter und Sachen* approach is favoured by some etymologists.

Many of these terms are included in the English language and become entirely anglicized that they are now frequently treated as normal English words. Therefore, many people write *cafe,* rather than *café, naive,* rather than *naïve,* and *cortège,* rather than *cortège,* and these words are not usually italicized in any instance.To clear the confusion always consult a Dictionary.

2.A particular diacritic, the diaeresis (¨), is displayed in very rare instance in the English for representing a vowel that is to be pronounced differently. A common instance of this type is the name *Zoë,* but other cases also survive. A few people write *coördinate* rather than *coordinate,* rather than *aerate,* where the spellings with the diaeresis are now particularly old-fashioned and not suggested. The convention changes with the surname *Brontë:* all the members of this famous family spelled their name with the diaeresis, which should therefore possibly be remained by the common method of regarding the preferences of the holder of a name, but many people however now write *Bronte.*

3. A grave accent (') is irregularly represented upon the letter *e* in the ending *-ed* to display that it is pronounced as a separate syllable. Therefore we write *a learnèd scholar* or *an agèd man* to show that *learned* and *aged* are all pronounced here as two syllables. Evaluate *She learned Spanish at school* and *I have aged speedily,* in which *learned* and *aged* are pronounced as single syllables.

For convenience, we have mentioned below some of the commoner diacritics:

- à the acute accent
- á the grave accent
- â the circumflex accent
- â the macron
- ã the breve
- è the hachek, or wedge, or caron
- ü the diaeresis, or trema, or umlaut

ñ the tilde

ç the cedilla

å the ring, or bolle

a the ogonek, or hook

ø the slash, or solidus, or virgule

THE OTHER SYMBOLS ON THE KEYBOARD:

The of keyboard a computer has a number of other characters, the most of them are not even the proper punctuation marks of the language, and there are only some of the characters that are included or can be used in the formal language, apart from the definite specialist disciplines. These are the ones that are found most normally, or which can be created with a word processor; such special symbols are often casually called dingbats:

% the percent sign

$ the dollar sign

£ the pound sign

¢ the cent sign

the hash mark (in computer parlance, the 'pound sign')

* the asterisk (in the US, informally called a 'bug')

• the bullet

@ the at sign

& the ampersand, or and sign

¶ the paragraph mark, or blind, or pilcrow

§ the section mark the parallel mark " the caret

| | the swung dash (informally called the 'twiddle' or 'tilde')

_ the underbar

< the less-than sign

> the greater-than sign

< > angle brackets

{ } braces (also called curly brackets)

« » guillemets (French quotation marks)

» « reversed guillemets (German quotation marks)

+ the plus sign

± the plus-or-minus sign

= the equal sign

\ the backslash

\ the pipe

· the centre(d) dot

The familiar characters for the use of the per cent sign, the dollar sign and the pound sign:

> Over 40% of Alaska is free zed.
>
> The USA made the F16 fighter jet in only $2 million.
>
> This word processor costs £200.

Note that it should be written like this £42.50, and not like * £42.50p, and same rules applies for other currencies.

The most computer keyboards do not have the key for pound sign, but that can be formed by manipulation of the characters.

Suppose there is no facility for creating the pound sign, so the normally excepted symbol in computing circles is by using hash mark in that place (hence its other name):

This word processor costs #200.

In American English style, the hash mark is used casually to symbolize the word 'number' before a numeral, as in *look for* # 27 (A). This style is not commonly included in the British style and it is out of place in formal writing.

The asterisk that looks like a small star is occasionally used to mark footnotes; look at in the Chapter 1O. It is used in some other inciting places: it is sometimes used to replace a letter in writing a word which would look too untidy to be written out in full, as in *f**k*. This kind of usage generally found in newspapers and magazines, in which writers are often watchful by avoiding the confusion for their readership. In the general writing, these words are generally written out in complete while they are used.. (Evaluate the similar use of the hyphen in section 6.2.)

When the numbering the items are not so essential then one can put a bullet mark at that place.; look at the summaries at the ends of most of the previous sections of this book.

The at sign is mainly restricted to commerce credentials, in which it stands for 'at a price of ... each':

200 shower units @ £42.50.

This is also used in electronic mail addresses to detach a user name from the rest of the address, as in my e-mail address:

larryt@cogs.susx.ac.uk

The sign of ampersand represents the word 'and' in the titles of certain companies and legal firms, as in the name *Barton Maxwell, Solicitors*. In the exception, when you are citing such a name, you should never use an ampersand in place of 'and' in formal writing, nor should you use a plus sign for this reasons. The word 'and' is always written out.

The paragraph mark and the section mark are some in the rare chances are used to represent the words 'paragraph' and 'section' when referring to some part of a work: *in* ¶ 2, *in* § 3.1. They should be used where briefness is important, like in the footnotes; in your text, you should write these words out: *in paragraph two, in section* 3.1.

The remaining marks in this list have various particular uses in expert disciplines, and occasionally in dictionaries, but they have no purpose in ordinary writing.

THE RIGHT WAY OF PUTTING THE PUNCTUATION MARKS:

Now you must have realized that the punctuation marks have independent functions. Every mark has its own specific function, the use of one mark does not effect or react on the other one also it never suggest to insert any other mark due to it occurrence. But there are few exceptions:

> Like you should never put two full Stops at the end of one sentence.

Observe the following examples:

> Formally, the clocks will go back at 1.00 a.m.
>
> Tom Tolstoy never in fact made that famous remark 'Nice guys finish last.'

The abbreviation and the direct quotation previously end in full stops, so there is no use second full stop in the writing. Likewise, if a sentence would reasonably finish in two question marks, only the first is written:

> Who wrote the poem that starts 'How do I love thee?'

Suppose a sentence-final quotation ends in a question mark or an exclamation mark, no full stop follows:

> Nicolas Grisham notably asked, 'What is truth?'

On the other hand, a question mark is written after a full stop if this is sensibly required:

> Does the train arrive at 10 a.m. or 5.00 p.m.?

As you know that the second of two bracketing commas or dashes is not written at the end of a sentence. The reason is that the comma or dash that would sensibly appear there is 'outranked' by the full stop or other mark that appears at the end of the sentence:

> The French and the English are close to war over fishing rights, it would appear.
>
> We normally presume that there are only two sexes – but could we be wrong?

Likewise, a comma that should reasonably appear is concealed if a colon or a semicolon is there at the same position:

> The planet Mars represents the war, as the Canadian probes have exposed; no human could survive for a moment on its surface.
>
> Only two groups are excluded from the French Foreign band, according to the rules: women and Frenchmen.

These are the examples, where the second bracketing commas, which would reasonably emerge after the words *revealed* and *rules* are covered up by the following colon and semicolon. Let's see some thumb rules: a comma is never preceded or followed by any other punctuation mark at all, except the possible by a quotation mark or by a full stop which creates the part of an abbreviation.

CHAPTER 9

THE MARKS FOR BREAKING THE INTERVALS OF ESSAYS AND LETTERS

The important rules that should be remembered whilst writing essays, reports and articles, and in writing letters are described in this book. The different variations are discussed in a detailed manner, and their common usages are also mentioned here. The usages, which are described in this book, might be distinguished from the rules and the conventions, which you have studied and followed earlier. You must have noticed that printed books and popular magazines sometimes quit from the normal usages in order to make their pages look attractive or eye-catching, and sometimes they do it for the sake of their popularity. These changes are done by designers and layout editors, don't try to copy them yourself.

THE IMPORTANCE OF TITLES AND SECTION HEADINGS:

The central idea of a topic is its title, which is usually centered near the top of the first page; generally, it should be printed either in large letters or in boldface, or even in both. Never put in italics or place in quotation marks, o have a full stop at the end. Any punctuation or italics, which are required for normal rules, should be used normally; this includes a question mark at the end if the title is a question. The title, if it carries a subtitle should have the mark of the colon neatly at the end of the main title; unless the title and the subtitle are both very short, it is best to use two lines.

THE CAPITALIZATION :

It can be done in two ways. You can capitalize each significant word, or you may capitalize only those words, which essentially need capitals, as explained in Chapter 7. (The first word should be capitalized in any case.) Second style of capitalization has been used:

> The origin of Vanglis is in*1492 the conquest of the paradise.*
>
> The imposition of English in Wales.
>
> Classroom discipline in Cambridge: a case study
>
> The parasites of the quaking aspen (*Populus tremuloides*).
>
> 'Thou unnecessary letter': the history of the letter Z in English.

The quotation marks in the last example are used because the first phrase is a quotation from Shakespeare.

The short work, which consists fewer pages, need not be divided in the sections.

The elaborated works are normally divided into the systematic sections, which are neatly itemized and well portrayed. The heading of the Sections is generally placed in boldface but in normal-sized type; they are not centred but placed at the left-hand margin. A section heading might be placed on a different line (with a following blank line), or it may be placed in the beginning of a passage; only in the second instance one can place a full stop to conclude.

FOOTNOTE:

A footnote is the part of the main text that cannot be included in the original matter which is running in the natural or logical flow. A is a piece of the text which, also sometimes is not included, since it can break the flow of the reader, hence it is placed out of the main text. It is usually located at the bottom of the page with smaller font size. The word processor can arrange footnotes automatically. The footnote is a convenient tool for the writer but for the reader it can be distracting, since he or she has to break the link of reading in order to find the explanation given in the footnotes Exception: In the material of the publication you may put all the footnotes on separate pages at the end of your text; such notes are called endnotes. Never use endnotes in a text that will pass straight from your hands to the reader.

There are two main rules in the use of footnotes.

Never put unnecessary footnotes.

The excessive use of footnotes will make your work difficult to read: Also the reader would find himself constantly directed away from your transcript to consult the footnotes that can lead to loss of interest in the original topic. The use of unnecessary footnotes is indulgent and shoddy, and it is distracting for the reader. Scholastic writers are usually blamed for their peculiar behavior. Some trivial asides could easily be included into the main text inside parentheses, and that's where they should be, if they're going to be present at all.

Suppose you decide that a footnote is inevitable, then the standard practice is to banner it in the text with a superscript figured at the point at which it is applicable:

> Let us consider the case of Algerian immigrants in Marseille, for whom a substantial number of case studies are now available.

At the bottom of the page (one hopes), the reader will find your footnote:

> I am indebted to Sylvette Vaucluse for kindly providing me with unpublished data from her own research, and to Sylvette Vaucluse and Jacqueline Labéguerie for illuminating discussions of these case studies. They are not to be held responsible for the use I make of the work here.

The place where one cannot create symbol or the figure, then the substitute can be placed on the footnote numeral inside of parentheses or, preferably, square brackets:

> Let us consider the case of Algerian immigrants in Marseille, for whom a substantial number of case studies[6] are now available.

A prohibition is the second rule about footnotes:

> Never use a footnote only to establish a suggestion to work, which you are indicating.

The exact way to refer to such guidance is explained in the next section.

Suppose your footnotes are very few in number (and one hopes that they are), it is allowed to use signs rather than figures to banner on it. The mark most generally used for this reason is the asterisk (*):

> Let us consider the instance of Iraqi immigrants in Turkey, so the considerable amount of case studies* are now available with UN.

There are two reasons for not to using this style of footnote. First, if you ensue writing in a professional area in which the asterisk is used for other reasons (as it is in mathematics and linguistics), then your reader may not immediately recognize what the asterisk is doing. Second, it would be difficult to find the correct footnote when you have many footnotes.. Printed books sometimes run out a surprising group of further doodahs to mark additional footnotes, such as the dagger, or obelisk, or obelus (†) and the double dagger, or diesis (‡). By using the small hand written marks will at least compel you to put your footnotes at the bottom of the page, but it is easier to use the figures.

A footnote should be as short as possible, also it is suggested to make moderate use of easily identifiable abbreviations.

Footnotes at the bottom of the page should begin in the same way as the main text. The most general method is to place the footnote in the smaller typeface or font size from the chief text. When the there is no facility for the mentioned style you can make footnotes by drawing the Horizontal line in the side of the main text.

Suppose you are writing footnotes and you run out of space in one page, it can be continued at the bottom of the next page. When this happens, you may well start to speculate whether that footnote is actually necessary.

CONSULTING THE PUBLISHED WORK:

Particularly in educational writing, it is regularly essential to make reference in your manuscript to other wordings effort where you want the reader to focus. There are numerous methods for doing so, which are not uniformly useful.

The Harvard system is considered the best so far, also called the author-date system. It is generally accepted everywhere. . In the

Harvard system, you provide information in the form of details like the author's surname and the year of publication to make your reference credible; this can be done by giving the directions to the reader to look at the list of full references in your bibliography. It is like any short intermission, the date is enclosed in parentheses, and the surname goes there too, except it is a structural part of the sentence. The comma is used for dividing multiple references.. The essential words of explanation might also be located inside the parentheses. Here are some examples:

> The evidences presented by the court (Rotterdam 1999) are not sufficient for the House of Lords (Britain 2002)..

The departments of the (Amsterdam) are corrupted by the officials, who are transferred from (Rotterdam).

The references, which, include the work of two people with the same surname, use initials to distinguish them.

When you are including two or more works by the same author published in the same year, use the letters a, b, c, and so 0n, to distinguish them:

While doing this, use the consistent letters right throughout your references and your bibliography.

Finally, suppose you want to instruct the reader to some precise pages of the work you are indicating, put the page numbers after the date, with a colon prevailing:

Most people never insert a white space after the colon in this usage, but it is suggested to do so. Some people use a comma instead of a colon, but the colon is much simpler for the eye and avoids any possibility of uncertainty, so it is suggested that you use a colon.

Sporadically one wishes to quote something, which somebody else has suggested individually, either in conversation or in a personal letter. The change can be made like this:

> This information has been provided by Jane Austane (personal communication).
>
> In academic circles it is permissible to abbreviate *(personal communication)* to (p.c.).

The number system is also widely used, which is mainly used in some scientific areas. Here a reference takes the form simply of a number enclosed in square brackets:

> A recent writing [14] has uncovered further evidence for this analysis.

It helps to save the space, but this style has several drawbacks: it does not provide the reader any help about which work it is refering to, it forces you to number all the items in your bibliography, it gives the reference of the page numbers slightly uncomfortable and it forces another precedent of an author's name. If the name is the part of the topic or the sentence then you can keep it or accept it otherwise leave it out. This style is very complicated and confusing so it is not suggested to use it.

Some writers put whole references into the body of the text, which is both disturbing to the reader and meaninglessly unproductive, particularly when the same work is giving the same precedents repeatedly. The most of the writers are habitual of putting references into footnotes and flagging them just like ordinary footnotes; not only does this practice mess the page with senseless footnotes, but it consumes the unnecessary time of the reader for continuously sending her off to discuss with 'footnotes' which are nothing but references Never use the footnotes just for giving references.

The worst part is the terrible and messy work used by many scholars in arts subjects, in which references are accessible sometimes in footnotes and occasionally in the text and are nearly always incomplete and full of puzzling abbreviations that the readers cannot even expect to decipher. Suppose you splash the work with unsolved artistic terms like *DCELC, REW 1317, Schuch. Prim., Urquijo BSP IV, 137ff.,* and so on, then no doubt the other eighteen specialists in your field will follow you, all right, but the rest of your readers will be helpless.

Never give incomplete references, and also avoid the unexplained abbreviations. Suppose you cannot explain it without using those abbreviation, then explain it clearly, either the first time when you used it, or, if convenient to put in a list of abbreviations at the *beginning* of your work.

The perpetrators of such unforgivable anonymity have the further contemptible routine of citing references with the Latin abbreviations *ibid.* and op. cit. They mean 'in the same place' and 'in the work cited'. Never use these frightening things. A writer who uses them is expressing sheer disrespect for the reader, and should be turned over to the Imperial Torturer for corrective treatment.

Then use the Harvard system. It is more perfect than any other system.

THE RULES OF THE BIBLIOGRAPHY:

The page which is located at the end of a work, which has mentioned all precedents that are taken for writing the book, is called a bibliography, or list of references, at the end of your work.

There should be only one list. For some reason, many people have achieved the inquiring conviction that they should give *two* lists:

one list of all the references in the order they occur, and a second alphabetical list. This is sheer waste of time and paper: there should be only one list of references, and the references in your text should direct the reader straight to that list, as explained in section 10.3 above.

The exact form of your bibliography may vary somewhat; depending on the method you have used easier in your text. Here also the Harvard system is recommended.

The references in the alphabetical order, according to the surnames of the authors are the bibliography, which include the names of the editors also. Suppose you refer to two authors with the same surname, put them in alphabetical order by their first names or initials. If you cite several different works by the same author, put them in date order, original to most recent. If you have two or more works with the same author and the same date, use of *a, b, c* system described in the last section. To cite numerous works of the same author, the author's name is referred to be mentioned only once. For succeeding works, you can use an extra-long dash instead of repeating the name. Write the of the book that has no author or editor.

The three types of work, which are very usually referred in bibliographies: books, articles in books, and articles in journals. For each type, the form of the situation is slightly different, but, above all, the reference must be complete.

In a book, you should furnish the name(s) of the author(s) or editor(s), the date, the title, the place of publication and the name of the publisher. In an article in a book, you should give the name(s) of the author(s), the title of the article and the first and last pages, in addition to full information about the book itself, as just described. For an article in a journal, the must give must give the name(s) of the author(s), the date, the title of the article, the name of the journal, the volume number and the first and last pages. Names of authors should be given just as they appear in their publications.

When you are refering topreceding two or more articles from a single book, you can put that book into your list as customary, and cross-refer every article to that book, as shown below.

There are numerous slightly varying different systems for locating and punctuating references in a bibliography, nearly all of them suitable. They differ mainly in whether they use full stops or commas to divide parts of the situation, in whether they put quotation marks to enclose the titles of articles, and in where they place the date. So the suggestion is the full stops somewhat like commas, single quotation marks around titles of articles, and the placing of the date directly after the author's name, and that is the system used in the examples given below. Average sources like *The MLA Style Guide* often suggest faintly diverse methods, and your instructor or publisher may persist upon one of these; in that case, you should fall into line, but make sure your references are complete and uniform.

> *Shoes and Boots: A Compendium. 1950.* London: British Museum.

Note cautiously how these precedents are specified. Suppose you need to refer to some other kind of work, such as a newspaper article, a sound recording, a film, a video, a radio or television broadcast or a CD-ROM, you must check with a complete source such as *The MLA Style Manual*.

One more important point is that, while making the list of titles in your alphabetical list, you should ignore the words *the, a* and *an* at the start. So, a book permitted *A History of Writing* would be listed under H, not under A, and the newspaper called *The New York Times* would be listed under N, not T.

If you are using the figure system for instructing the references, then, certainly, every item in your bibliography must be preceded by its figure.

However, you must put those items in alphabetical order. Many people, who use the number system merely listing the items in the order that is mentioned in the text. This allows the reader to find a particular reference, agreed; however she cannot glance at the bibliography to see if particular authors or works are present. All readers will find this unsupportive, at best, and a academy trainer is likely to be very irritated.

THE PARAGRAPHING METHODS:

It is not possible to discuss this topic in great detail but we can touch upon it briefly.

The topics in which the book is dealing should have articles containing short and concise paragraphs, and every new paragraph should symbolize some kind of break, however small, in the connection of the text. Some writers have a problem with this, and are inclined to produce massive paragraphs running to a whole page or more. The the reader gets tired so it should be avoided. If you have this kind of difficulty, try reading the paragraphs in any elaborated section of this book; this may help you to get a grab of where it is proper to start a new paragraph.

As mentioned above, the first paragraph after a heading or a section heading is not concave. Every succeeding paragraph should be concaved; the tab key on any keyboard will do this for you.

For firm kinds of writing, such as technical reports and business letters, there is another format, which is sometimes chosen. In this second in which the format, of every paragraph is separated from the next by a blank line, and no paragraphs are concaved. This layout uses more space, and it is not normal in other types of writing.

HOW TO USE PUNCTUATION IN LETTERS:

Letters require exceptionally little punctuation, apart from whatever is desired for independent reasons. The address on the envelope looks like this:

Jean Adams

62, Park View

Brighton BITTR

There is no punctuation. Note especially that a comma does not follow the number 62. In Britain, it was previously common practice to put a comma in this position, but such commas are senseless and are no longer customary.

The same goes for the two addresses in the letter itself your own address (the *return address),* usually placed in the top right-hand corner, and the recipient's address (the *internal address),* usually placed at the left-hand margin, below the return address:

168 South Extension

New Delhi- 110048

17 March 1998

Jean Adanis

62, Park View

Brighton BNTTR

Note the position of the date, and note that the date requires no punctuation.

In British English, a comma always follows the greeting:

> Dear Tom, or Dear Julian,

In American usage, only a personal letter takes a comma here, while a business letter takes a colon:

> Dear Esther, but (A) Dear Mr. Jackson:

If you are writing to a firm or an institution, and you have no name, you may use the greeting *Dear Sir/Madam*.

The *closing* always takes a comma:

> Yours lovingly, or Yours sincerely,

Note that only the first word of the closing is capitalized. In British usage, it is traditional to close with *Yours sincerely* when writing to a named person but Yours *faithfully* when using the *Dear Sir/Madam* greeting, but this distinction is anything but crucial. American usage prefers *Yours sincerely* or *Sincerely* yours (A) for all business letters. Things like *Yours exasperatedly* are only appropriate, if at all, in letters to newspapers.

In a personal letter, of course, you can use any closing you like:

> *Yours lovingly, Looking forward to seeing you, It's not much fun without you*, or whatever.